AN ANSWER
IN DEFENCE OF THE TRUTH

AGAINST THE

APOLOGY OF PRIVATE MASS.

BY T. COOPER,
AFTERWARDS BISHOP,
FIRST OF LINCOLN, AND THEN OF WINCHESTER.

PUBLISHED IN 1562.

TO WHICH IS PREFIXED

(AS IN THE ORIGINAL EDITION)

THE WORK ANSWERED, ENTITLED

AN APOLOGY OF PRIVATE MASS,

AN ANONYMOUS POPISH TREATISE
AGAINST BISHOP JEWEL.

EDITED FOR

The Parker Society,

BY THE

REV. WILLIAM GOODE, M.A., F.S.A.,
RECTOR OF ALLHALLOWS THE GREAT AND LESS, LONDON.

Wipf & Stock
PUBLISHERS
Eugene, Oregon

Wipf and Stock Publishers
199 W 8th Ave, Suite 3
Eugene, OR 97401

An Answer in Defence of the Truth against
the Apology of Private Mass
By Cooper, Thomas and Jewel, John
ISBN: 1-59752-203-1
Publication date 5/18/2005
Previously published by Cambridge, 1850

ADVERTISEMENT.

THE work here reprinted is one which is not merely interesting from its great rarity and its connexion with the controversy raised by Bishop Jewel's famous challenge to the Papists, but of importance from its intrinsic excellence. Of the Author of the Popish Treatise prefixed, entitled *An Apology of private Mass*, (which seems to have been circulated only in MS. until it was printed in this work in conjunction with the *Answer*,) I am unable to give any account, having failed in discovering any intimation of the name of the writer. The reply to it which follows, entitled *An Answer in defence of the truth, against the Apology of private Mass*, has been sometimes attributed to Bishop Jewel; as for instance, in the Bodleian Catalogue, Oxon. 1738 (under *Missa*), and from hence by Watt in his "Bibliotheca Britannica," and (probably on the same authority) by Dr Jelf, in his recent edition of the works of Bishop Jewel, (see Vol. IV. p. 201 and Vol. V. p. 62.) The words of the Preface, however, in which Jewel is spoken of as "a worthy learned man and bishop of this realm," prove that this is a mistake. The real author was Thomas Cooper, then fellow of St Mary Magdalen College, Oxford, and afterwards successively bishop of Lincoln and Winchester. This fact we learn from the following passage, in a work by Dr E. Cradocke, Margaret Professor of Divinity at Oxford, published only ten years after, that is, in 1572, when Dr Cooper was bishop of Lincoln:—

"Being fully determined to write, upon the matter, notwithstanding, whereupon I might fitliest ground my process, I was not by and by resolved. Sometimes it came into my mind to take in hand some controversy of this time. But considering with myself what great learning hath been lately shewed in such questions, I was quickly changed from that mind. For what could any body now write of, for the improving or defending of such things, which very plentifully already hath not been discoursed? Would a man gladly be instructed touching the use of images? Let him peruse D. Calfchil's book against Martial. Would he hear what can be said of the Mass? Not only Master Dean of Paul's his books against Dorman are to be seen, but also the Treatise of the right reverend father Bishop Cowper, entitled, *The defence of the truth against the Mass*, and the works of the late famous bishop of worthy memory, D. Jewel; who in two of his great volumes hath gone through with so many and so profound matters of religion, that, for divers needful points to be spoken of, they might well serve a divine for common-place books." (E. Cradocke's Ship of assured safety ... containing in four books a discourse of God's Providence. Lond. Bynneman, 1572. 12mo. Epistle Dedic. to the Earl of Leicester, dated May 19, 1572, p. 4.)

For this reference I am indebted to Bishop Tanner, who in his "Bibliotheca Britannico-Hibernica," (Lond. 1748, fol. p. 198.) ascribes the treatise to Bishop Cooper, on the authority of this passage.

The testimony of Cradocke is so decisive, that it seems hardly necessary to refer to any other authorities; but it may be added, that Dr Fulke also in his "Catalogue of all such Popish books either answered or to be answered," &c., prefixed to his work entitled, "D. Heskins, D. Sanders and M. Rastel... overthrown and detected," &c. (Lond. 1579, 8vo.) notices the treatise thus,—" A defence of the private Masse, answered (by conjecture) by M. Cooper, Bishop of Lincoln;" which testimony he repeats in a similar Catalogue prefixed to his work entitled, "T. Stapleton and Martiall (two Popish Heretics) confuted," &c. Lond. 1580, 8vo.

Not having, as a Cambridge divine, the same opportunity of information as Dr Cradocke, who was of the same University as Bishop Cooper and a contemporary, Dr Fulke naturally speaks with the uncertainty of one who is only giving the testimony of common report.

The testimony of Fulke is quoted, as shewing that Bishop Cooper is probably the author of the work, by Thomas Baker, in his notes on Wood's Athenæ Oxon. (see Wood's Athen. Oxon. ed. Bliss, Vol. I. col. 612), and by Placcius in his Theatrum Anon. et Pseudon. ed. Hamb. 1708. fol. Tom. I. p. 516.

The work is noticed by Herbert, in his edition of Ames's Typographical Antiquities, (Vol. II. p. 875,) where the titles exactly correspond with those of the book here reprinted, excepting that Herbert has accidentally omitted, in the first title, the line " order appoincted in the." But he adds,—" The orthography of this differing so considerably from Mr Ames's copy, has the appearance of two editions in the same month." The following is the title as given by Ames:

" An apologie of the private masse, sediciously spread abroad in writing, without name of the author; as it seemeth against the offer and protestacion made in certain sermons, by the reverende father, byshop of Salesburie; with an answere and confutation of the same apologie. Set foorth for the maintenance and defence of the trueth. Perused and allowed, by the reverent father in God, Edmonde, bishop of London, according to the queen's majesties injunctions. *Mense Nov.* 1562." (Ames's Typograph. Antiq. Lond. 1749, 4to. p. 305.)

The title is marked with an asterisk, indicating that the book was in his possession.

I am unable to account for this discrepancy in the description of the title, but am indisposed to think that there was more than one edition of the work. Possibly the title given by Ames may have been prefixed to some copies of the work, and then withdrawn for the other.

A copy of the work is in the University Library at Cambridge, and another (in a somewhat imperfect state) is in the Bodleian Library at Oxford. The copy from which the following reprint is taken, at the request of the Council of the Parker Society, is in my own possession, purchased at the sale of the library of the late Archdeacon Pott.

I subjoin a brief Biographical Notice of Bishop Cooper, and a list of his Works which I believe will be found more complete and accurate than those hitherto given.

W. G.

BIOGRAPHICAL NOTICE

OF

BISHOP COOPER.

THE following account is given of Bishop Cooper by Anthony a Wood, in his *Athenæ Oxonienses*.

"THOMAS COUPER or COOPER was born within the city of Oxon, educated in grammar learning in the school joining to St Mary Magdalen College, being then a chorister of that house; where with very great industry, making proficiency beyond his years, [he] was elected probationer in 1539, and in the year following perpetual fellow of the said house. Afterwards proceeding in the faculty of arts, he was made master of the school wherein he had been educated; left his fellowship about 1546, and gave himself solely up to the studies of Humanity and Medicine. In the reign of Queen Mary he, being then inclined to the Protestant religion, took, as it seems, a degree in Physic, and practised that faculty in Oxon; but when she was dead, he re-assumed his former faculty of Divinity, became a frequent preacher, took the degrees in that faculty in the latter end of 1566, being about that time made Dean of Christ Church in Oxon, and was several years after Vice-Chancellor of the University. In 1569, he was made Dean of Gloucester, in the place of John Man deceased, and in 1570, Feb. 24, he was consecrated Bishop of Lincoln. In 1584 he was translated to Winchester; where, as in most parts of the nation, he became much noted for his learning and sanctity of life. I have heard some reverend and ancient divines of this University say, (as they had heard it from others who knew the man,) that at what time Dr Cooper was to leave Oxon, to go to the see of Lincoln, he did humbly confess, in his farewell sermon to the University, That he was born of very mean parents in Cat Street, that he had undergone several mean and servile offices in Magdalen College, till by the favour of friends he was advanced to be fellow and schoolmaster, &c. And so going forward with a recital of the chief parts of his life, did, in conclusion, humbly acknowledge God's great providence towards him, praying withal, That he would be pleased to prosper him in that great employment which was put upon him, &c. Of this person much may be said, and perhaps some wrong might redound to his memory, if I should say little; for he was indeed a reverend man, very well learned, and exceeding industrious....The course of his life in Oxon was very commendable....At length this reverend and holy bishop, paying his last debt to nature at Winchester,

29 April, in 1594, was buried on the south side of the choir, a little above the bishop's seat belonging to the cathedral there. Over his grave was soon after laid a flat marble, with an inscription thereon in prose and verse, a copy of which you may read in *Hist. et Antiq. Univ. Oxon.* Lib. II. p. 197, a." (Athen. Oxon. ed Bliss, Vol. I. col. 608—612).

The following is a list of Bishop Cooper's Works:—

1. An Epitome of Chronicles, containing the whole discourse of Histories as well of this realm of England, as all other Countries...first by Thomas Lanquet, from the beginning of the world to the Incarnation of Christ, and now finished and continued to the reign of our sovereign Lord King Edward the Sixth, by Thomas Cooper. Lond. T. Berthelet, 1549. 4to. An edition surreptitiously put forth by some other hand, with additions, was published 1559. 4to. A second edition, by T. Cooper, continued to the death of Queen Mary, was published under the title of Cooper's Chronicle, Lond. T. Berthelet, 1560. 4to.; and a third, continued to the 7th year of Queen Elizabeth, in 1565, 4to.

2. Bibliotheca Eliotæ. Sive Dictionarium Lat. et Angl. auctum et emend. per Tho. Cooper, Lond. T. Berthelet, 1548. fol.—Eliot's Dictionary, the

second time enriched and more perfectly corrected, by Thomas Cooper, Schoolmaster of Maudlen's in Oxford. Lond. T. Berthelet, 1552. fol.—Eliot's Dictionary, by T. Cooper, the third time corrected, Lond. T. Berthelet, 1559. fol.

3. Thesaurus Linguæ Romanæ et Britannicæ... op. et ind. T. Cooperi Magdalenensis. Accessit Dictionarium Historicum et Poeticum, Lond. 1565. fol. Reprinted 1573, 1578, 1584. fol.

4. A Brief Exposition of such chapters of the Old Testament as usually are read in the Church at Common Prayer on the Sundays throughout the year. Lond. 1573. 4to.

5. True and perfect copy of a godly Sermon preached in the Minster at Lincoln, 28th Aug. 1575, on Matt. xvi. 26, 27. Lond. 1575. 16mo., 1619. 4to.

6. Articles to be enquired of within the Diocese of Lincoln, in the Visitation of Thomas, Bishop of Lincoln. Lond. R. Newbery, 1574.

7. Injunctions given by the Rev. Father in God, Thomas, Bishop of Lincoln, to be observed throughout his Diocese. Lond. R. Newbery, 1577.

8. Certain Sermons, wherein is contained the Defence of the Gospel now preached against cavils and false accusations, as are objected both against the doctrine itself and the preachers and professors thereof by the friends and favorers of the Church of Rome. Lond. 1580. 4to. These Sermons are twelve in number, and are on Rom. i. 16; Matt. vii.

15, 16; 1 Cor. x. 1, 3, 5; Matt. xiii. 3, 5; John viii. 46.

9. An Admonition to the People of England, wherein are answered not only the slanderous untruths reproachfully uttered by Martin the Libeller, but also many other crimes by some of his brood objected generally against all Bishops, and the chief of the Clergy, purposely to deface and discredit the present state of the Church. Lond. 1589. 4to. There were two editions of this work in the same year, 1589, in the second of which, though having precisely the same title, and no notice of being a second edition, various alterations were made. The second edition was reprinted, Lond. 1847, 8vo. The work was published anonymously, but is well known to be Bishop Cooper's, and has the initials T. C. at the end of the Preface.

To these must be added (on the authority of the evidence given in the foregoing "Advertisement") the work here reprinted, namely,—

10. An Answer in defence of the truth against the Apology of Private Mass. Lond. 1562. 12mo.

Both Bishop Tanner in his *Bibliotheca Britannico-Hibernica*,(Lond. 1748, fol.) and Dr Bliss in his edition of Wood's *Athenæ Oxonienses*, add to these the following:—

Homilies on the Seven Sacraments, 1558.

But this is clearly a mistake, as Bishop Cooper was then engaged in medical pursuits, and moreover was a Protestant. The work referred to is the following:—Holsome and Catholike Doctrine concerning the Seven Sacraments of Chrystes Church. Lond. 1558, 4to., which is by Thomas Watson, then Bishop of Lincoln, but deprived on the accession of Queen Elizabeth. The mistake has no doubt arisen from both authors having the name, "Thomas, Bishop of Lincoln."

Of MSS. of Bishop Cooper remaining, Bishop Tanner (in the work above quoted) gives the following account:—

"*Oxoniensis Academiæ gratulationem de adventu serenissimæ reg. Elizabethæ ad ædes comitis Leycestrensis, cancellarii acad. coram eadem pronunciatam a T. Cooper*. Pr. 'Mirum fortasse tibi videri,' &c. MS. C. C. C. Oxon. Twin. IV. et MS. bibl. reg. Westmon. 12. A. XLVII. *Librum ordinationum et decretorum pro coll. S. M. Magd. Oxon. factorum et institutorum* per T. Cooperum epis. Winton. dat. 17 Octob. MDLXXXV. *Christianam cum fratribus consultationem, utrum pii verbi ministri præscriptam a magistratibus vestium rationem suscipere et liquido possint et inire debeant*. Pr. ded. M. Parkero, Archiep. Cant. 'Quod semel atque iterum postulasti.' MS. C. C. C. Cantabr. Miscell. F. p. 135. [CCCXL. 7. p. 354. Nasmith's Cat.]...*Epistolam M. Parkero*. [dat. Jan. 4, 1568.] MS. C. C. C. Cantabr. Miscell. 839. [CXIV. 306, p. 166. Nasm. Cat.]"

To these Dr Bliss, in his edition of Wood's *Athe-*

næ Oxonienses, (I. 612, 613,) adds the following:—
"Original Letters from him, MSS. Cotton., Vespasian, F. xi. fol. 187, dated June 14, 1586; Otho, E. xi. fol. 196, January 25 and 27, 1587-8. The last, concerning the musters of his diocese, to the Earl of Essex, then Lord Lieutenant of Hants."

W. G.

AN APOLOGY

OF

PRIVATE MASS.

An Apologie

of priuate Masse, spred a
broade in writing without name
of the authour: as it seemeth, a-
gainst the offer and protestacion
made in certayne Sermons by
the reuerent father Bisshop of
Salsburie: with an answer to
the same Apologie, set foorth
for the maintenance and
defence of the
trueth.

Perused and allowed, by the reuerent
father in God Edmonde Bisshop
of London, accordynge to the
order appoincted in the
Queenes maiestes
Iniunctions.

LONDINI.
Mens. Nouemb.
1562.

AN APOLOGY

OF

PRIVATE MASS.

HAVING heard by sundry sufficient reports of large offers in open places before right honourable audience, more stoutly, as wise men think, than clerkly, for the maintenance of divers untruths: and that the learned of the clergy here stand bound in recognizance, not to gainsay any doctrine now preached, which otherwise are well able to control all such erroneous fancies lately devised: notwithstanding I am nothing comparable to the learned of the clergy, yet, being brought up in learning always beyond the seas, having before mine eyes the fear of God, and mine heart greatly lamenting to see error outface the truth, thought it good for the discharge of mine own conscience before God and you, to discover certain vanities of yours, that the catholic church (once your mother) misliketh in you. And so much the rather, because God of his infinite goodness hath called me back again from all such lewd fancies, by the godly instruction of the learned: in the which I was once so fully persuaded by evil books, that all that time I neither regarded God, nor good religion, nor any good conscience besides. And therefore, trusting to do some good with such as simplicity without malice hath persuaded to stay, conscience pricked me to give the adventure: nothing doubting but that God will bring that to a good end, the beginning whereof had no evil meaning.

CAP. I.
Against his refusal in the first Epistle to D. Cole.

A.

And to make mine entry with you, master Jewel, which are counted the greatest clerk on your side, I marvel not a little why you, being reputed a man of such learning, utterly refuse to prove the doctrine you teach; alleging very slender causes of your refusal, that serve the contrary side, rather than yours. Your vocation to so high a room, the place where you taught, the honourable estate of the audience which heard you, the doctrine you taught, authorised by the realm, as you allege, do not unburden you from the proof of your doctrine, but rather burden you more to prove the same; because your estate is now such, that is bound to render account of that you teach. Nor is it any dishonour to the realm, if you be able to certify that by learning, that they (as you say) have passed by laws; nor want of discretion at all in you to teach them, that would so gladly learn at your hand. For if a man may prove by conference of scriptures any article therein comprised, either in the letter, or by argument bolted forth, without any dishonour to God, or blemish to him that taketh the matter in hand (as a man indeed may); shall you count the realm dishonoured, or want of discretion in yourself, to prove such doctrine (as yourself do publish), because it is authorised by man, and by the assent of the realm? which in time of your baptism assented to the contrary, as all other christian realms did, without any contradiction at all, amongst the learned: whereas in this assent, as many learned clerks, well-known to the world, said nay, and more too, than hitherto hath said yea. And if the chief proof of your doctrine be the assent of this realm, shall not other christian realms, that teach quite contrary unto you, rest in doctrine authorised by them and all christian realms besides? Here you are driven, if you rest so stoutly upon the assent of realms, to confess that the doctrine taught here is true, because this realm hath authorised it: and the doctrine in strange realms is true, being quite contrary to yours, because by like reason the realms there hath authorised it. You have no refuge in this case, but to say, that this realm followed the scripture in such doctrine as they authorised, and that other realms followed not the scripture in authorising the contrary. I am well contented with your answer. But where be the scriptures whereby the realm authorised your doctrine? You may not say, it shall be great dishonour to the realm, to have such scriptures known, for want of discretion in you to utter them: as you seem to say in your letters. Let us know such scriptures as your trust is most upon, to prove your doctrine by, and we will depart quietly. And as all wise men will count it the office of a discreet man, either to stay such as stagger, or to persuade such as verily think otherwise: so shall I not only so think, but also, if you give me good cause why, yield you great thanks, and my poor service too. In your silence herein, if you have ought to say, you shall do nothing else but hide the candle under the bushel: whereas the order is to set it upon the candlestick, to light all such as are within the house. If you have no scriptures to lay for you, then trouble our mother the holy catholic church no longer.

You stand in negatives: you say against private masses and certain other, which, as you pretend, cannot be proved. Have we not here good cause to marvel that you, which study so marvellous reformation of all doctrine to the touchstone of scripture, will openly profess, bearing such a personage in such places of honour, such doctrine as can neither be proved by scripture, nor any other substantial record: and all because it standeth in negatives? May not children in this sort devise negatives containing false doctrine, and when they are called upon to prove it, say they are not bound to prove their assertions, because they are negatives? This dare I be bold to say: if you had sentence, or half sentence, word, or half word in the scriptures, old doctors, general councils, or example of the primitive church against private masses, all England had rung of it ere this day. But you have none, as your silence importeth. It were either great folly to keep that secret, the which without any damage may do good to many, or marvellous envy to enclose

B.

Against his staying upon the negative.

that without gain, which law and reason would have to be common. *Quicquid dando non deficit* (saith St Austin), *quamdiu habetur, et non datur, nondum habetur, quomodo habendum est*[1]. "All that decay not by bestowing, as long as they are had, and not bestowed, they are not yet had, as they ought to be had." The laws may in divers special facts, not restrained to time and place, teach perhaps, that a negative cannot be proved. But to say that a negative in doctrine, as yours is, cannot be proved upon only consideration that it is a negative, as your shift is, that I am well assured no learned man hitherto ever taught; either in law, or in any other science besides. Yea, the contrary rather appeareth in logic: the which teacheth the general grounds of all disputations. Where we have in every figure, negative conclusions. And for other short kind of arguments, there are as many places dialectical of the negatives to destroy, as there are affirmatives to build on. So that shift of descant cannot serve your turn. Doth not the scripture many times join issue in the negative, and prove the same? We are not justified by Moses' law, and so the like. Doth not the apostles prove it at large?

But forasmuch as you are not able to prove the negative, I will no further trouble you therewith. Yet, when there is an af-

[1 Omnis enim res quæ dando non deficit, dum habetur et non datur, nondum habetur quomodo habenda est.—AUG. De doctr. Christ. Lib. I. c. 1. Tom. III. p. 1. col. 5. Op. ed. Ben. Paris. 1689, et seq.]

firmative implied in the negative, as there is here, though I discharge you of very gentleness from the proof of the one, order of schools will drive you to prove the other: though it were in facts, much more in doctrine.

CAP. II.

A distinction of private.

A.

Your negative was, that there was no private mass at all in the primitive church; thus you say, and shew no cause why. This term private, which you in this place first invented, I mean Luther's school, may be taken concerning this matter divers ways. One way, private is contrary to common, to many. And in this signification, we never said that any mass was private. For the catholic church ever taught, that the mass is a common or public sacrifice, restrained to none so, but that the whole church, or any lively member thereof, had thereby great commodity; and might, being prepared, and well-disposed, be partaker, not only of the Common Prayer and Suffrages offered up to God in the mass, but also of the holy sacrament of Christ's body and blood therein consecrated and offered. We never yet prisoned up the holy sacrifice of the mass, or the sacrament therein received, or the use of any of them, from any that disposed themselves godly. If you had heard us preach that the mass is only available to the priest, or to princes, or to us of England, or to them of Italy, or to men, and not to women, or to such as are alive, and not to such as are dead, or to say that none ought to receive the sacrament but the priest, you might have charged us that we went about to enclose that to some one sort of private profit, that ought to remain in common for all sorts of people. And in this wise we never taught, that any mass was private.

B. But you have the other signification of this term private: that is, the sole receiving of the sacrament by the priest, embarring none to communicate with him, yea, rather rejoicing, if any would be so well disposed to receive with him; and lamenting, when he seeth the people so evil disposed, that none will order themselves so, that they may worthily receive with him; and yet not forcing them to receive, when they are not disposed, nor ready. And in this meaning of private, the catholic church doth teach, that the priest may receive the sacrament at mass alone, when none other is disposed to receive with him. Now, if you be able, we require you to prove the affirmative included in your negative; which is this: That every priest, or any other, ought, when he receiveth the sacrament, to have company to receive with him in the same time and place, upon pain of God's high indignation: and then we will yield unto you. If you be able to prove neither the negative, nor the affirmative, storm not so sore against the doctrine of the catholic church, the which falsehood many times assaulteth, and was never yet able to overthrow.

CAP. III. As you say, there was no private mass in the primitive church, and say untruly, so may you say and say truly, there was no christian king in the apostles' time. There was no christian man that then counted anything his own of such things as he possessed; but all were common. There was then no doctrine taught, but it was confirmed by miracles. There was no woman that might come with open face to the church. There was no bishop endowed with temporalities. There was no distinction commonly of parishes. There was nothing eaten that was mingled with blood. There was no whole realms turned to the faith. There was no receiving of the sacrament, but after supper. There was no infant but was houselled. And thus may we roll in a great sort such, there was not, truly, as you roll in divers of yours, falsely. And will you, I beseech ye, reform all things to the very state of the primitive church now? Will you suppress all christian kings which were not in the apostles' time? Will you alter the state now, and make all things to be common? Will you disgrace all preachers that work not miracles? Will you enforce women to hoodwink themselves in the church? Will you rail against bishops that keep any temporalities? Will ye set men at liberty to do their duty at what church they will? Will ye inhibit the folks to eat bloodings, or pigeons, or capons, such as are killed by stifling? Will you enforce us to be houselled after supper? Will you housel all babes and infants again? To call such things to the state of the apostles' time, and of the primitive church again, is nothing else, but to enforce a tall

That all things should not be brought to the form of the primitive church.

B.
The primitive church the state of infancy.

man to come to his swaddling clothes, and to cry alarm in his cradle again. I trust when you say there was no private mass in the primitive church, notwithstanding you disallow private mass, yet you will allow mass to be in the primitive church: or else wisdom would have said more generally there was no mass at all, nor private, nor common, &c. And yet there is an open difference between these two sentences: there was no private mass at that time, and there ought to be no private mass at any time. In the one, we conceive the use of that age, notwithstanding the law of the church even then might stand indifferently to the contrary, upon circumstances and good considerations. And in the other, we precisely conceive what the law doth determine, either lawful or unlawful.

The constant faith, the pure life, the fervent charity, the contempt of the world, that then flourished so amongst such as professed Christ, might cause, perhaps, that no mass was celebrated, but that divers Christians, and specially looking for continual persecution, would be houselled thereat, and be always sure to have their *viaticum*, as it is termed in the old canons, that is to say, their voyage-provision. In that state of burning charity, and of contempt of the world, and all the pleasures thereof, some of the people, perhaps of their own accord, did always willingly and gladly prepare themselves at every mass to be houselled with the priest; and will you now in the state of key-cold charity, when the

C.

An argument of the comparison of the times.

people are nothing willing to dispose themselves to receive their housel, pluck the priest from the altar, whose office is to offer that daily sacrifice for the people, unless there be that will receive? Will you embar him that is bound to offer up the daily sacrifice of duty, because they will not dispose themselves to receive their housel? Who, as concerning so often receiving, are not bound, but stand at liberty. The church doth exhort them to the frequentation of their housel, but giveth no commandment to bind them: as Christ said, *Si vis perfectus esse, vade, et vende omnia quæ habes, et da pauperibus;* "If thou wilt be perfect, go and sell all that thou hast, and give it to the poor." Which implieth the nature of a counsel, to exhort men to the highest degree of christianity, concerning the bestowing of the goods of the world; and yet is no commandment to bind any that are not so disposed. Even so we may exhort and counsel folks to frequent the receiving of their rights without any commandment to bind them. Now the laymen are at liberty concerning the frequentation: the priest is bound to the frequentation. Is it then reason that he, that may choose whether he will frequently receive or no, should, when he is not disposed, cause him to offend the law of God that is bound thereto? If you had any such text in the holy scripture to bind the priest never to say mass without some to communicate, as this text: *Si vis perfectus esse, vade, vende,* seemeth to command him that will be perfect, to sell all that he hath, and bestow it upon the poor; Lord! how would ye then triumph: because you had then some colour against private mass. And yet when the matter were well bolted, you shall never be able to prove any commandment thereby against the sole receiving of the sacrament by the priest, but a counsel to exhort him, if it might be, to the highest and most perfect estate.

F.

But to prescribe of necessity that there ought, upon pain of God's indignation, to be a company to communicate with the priest at every mass, or else forbear the celebration of the holy sacrifice, having no tittle of any such colour in the holy scripture, I will not call that by the name that I may justly, but will temper the matter, and term it an itching folly, to alter all things that are well settled already.

St Chrysostom, in his Third Homily upon the Epistle to the Ephesians, in his complaint there doth so set forth the matter, as it is to be wished both what the people should do, and what the priest may do. If the people will not follow his exhortations, then no man, I suppose, without great impudency, will any longer stand in the denial thereof. For as we may well and godly wish that all folks were so well agreed that all suits in the law might surcease: and yet this godly wish, when any contention should chance, that cannot otherwise be finished, doth not inhibit but that men may sue for their right. For the highest or the perfectest state doth not extinguish the mean or the low: even so all good men may wish that all christian people were always so de-

CAP. IV.

A.
A similitude that company is not necessary.

vout and well disposed, that they might, with God's favour, receive their housel daily. And yet were it injury, because all will not, to inhibit such as would. Or if none would, to embar the priest that is bound to offer up the daily sacrifice for himself and the people.

The priest of duty bound to sacrifice.

CAP. V.
A.

St Chrysostom writeth thus: *In aliis quidem temporibus, quum puri frequenter sitis, non acceditis: in pascha vero, licet sit aliquid a vobis perpetratum, acceditis. O consuetudinem! O præsumptionem! sacrificium frustra quotidianum offerimus. Incassum assistimus altari, nullus est qui communicetur: hic non ut temere communicemini dico, sed ut vos dignos reddatis*[1]. "At other times," saith he, "although you be for the most part in clean life, you come not, but at Easter you come, though you have done somewhat amiss. Fie upon that custom, fie upon such presumption, the daily sacrifice is in vain. We stand at the altar for nought. There is none to be housled. I speak not these things because you should receive your housel rashly, but for the intent you should make yourselves worthy." In these words of St Chrysostom, this doth first appear, that at that time the people at Easter would receive their housel in what case soever they

[1 Ἐν μὲν τοῖς ἄλλοις καιροῖς οὐδὲ καθαροὶ πολλάκις ὄντες προσέρχεσθε, ἐν δὲ τῷ Πάσχα, κἂν ᾖ τι τετολμημένον ὑμῖν, πρόσιτε. ὢ τῆς συνηθείας, ὢ τῆς προλήψεως· εἰκῆ θυσία καθημερινή, εἰκῆ παρεστήκαμεν τῷ θυσιαστηρίῳ, οὐδεὶς ὁ μετέχων. ταῦτα οὐχ ἵνα ἁπλῶς μετέχητε, λέγω, ἀλλ' ἵνα ἀξίους ἑαυτοὺς κατασκευάζητε.—CHRYS. in Ephes. cap. 1. Hom. 3. Op. ed. Bened. Paris. Tom. XI. p. 23.]

were in, good or bad. And at other times of the year, though they were in good case and pure life, fit to receive, yet they would refrain the receiving of their rights. And therefore he blameth, and in manner crieth out upon that custom, whereby the people rather consider the prescript time of Easter to receive, than a clean life and pure conscience. For as godly people may at any time receive their housel, without restraint to any one prescript time in the year, and the oftener they so receive the same, the more their godly devotion thereby doth increase, even so the ungodly ones are rather commanded to do penance for their evil life, and to make themselves ready and worthy, than to come rashly without search of conscience, without trial of themselves, without penance done for their offences, to receive their housel only upon consideration of prescript time, because they had used of long time to do so. And this is the presumption he crieth out upon, that pricketh the people upon custom to receive unworthily: and yet at other times, where none would receive, neither such as might worthily, nor such as could not for their evil life, St Chrysostom saith, that there was *sacrificium quotidianum*. Every day daily sacrifice, every day mass, every day the priest stood at the altar, either to exhort such as were meet to receive, or to counsel such as were of evil lives to penance, that they after might be able to receive. But his exhortation was *incassum* at the altar. And his exhortation to the people to communicate in the celebration of

B.

the daily sacrifice was *frustra* in vain. Not for because the daily sacrifice in the mass was nothing available, but because he looked that the people would dispose themselves to do as they were exhorted. And that was vain, because *nullus est qui communicetur*. There was none that would be houselled. And yet the priest did celebrate notwithstanding. For it is said, that he standeth at the altar; and what to do but to celebrate the daily sacrifice? Can you call that a daily sacrifice that is not daily offered up? or that a daily

C. sacrifice that is not celebrated but once in the year, at Easter? At the which time the people used to receive: all other times they

D. refrained, *Quia nullus est qui communicetur*. "There is none to communicate." Is it not evident by this complaint of St Chrysostom, that the priest did his duty, notwithstanding there was none to receive with him? Or else if he were constrained to refrain when none would receive with him, doth it not appear, that then it followeth, that he did celebrate but at Easter only, for then he had company, and at other times he lacked. *Quia nullus est qui communicetur?* And then how could it be called *Sacrificium quotidianum*, 'the daily sacrifice?' Doubtless it could not. And therefore it is plain that then the priest did his duty in celebration of the mass, though none received with him. Have we not found then that in Chrysostom's time there was private mass, as you do term it?

Why say you, that, in all other things we hold contrary unto you, we had some colour other [either] in scriptures, or old doctors:

but in such doctrine as you made your entry upon, whereof this is one, you are assured we had no colour at all to make any proof in very deed. You hear that Chrysostom testifieth the use of his time for private mass, plainly and flatly without colour at all. What colour, I pray you, have you, either in scriptures, old doctors, or councils, against private mass? As it appeareth hitherto, nothing at all.

Your own principles, that such as ye are first invented, will drive you in manner to confess the catholic doctrine in this behalf. You say against prescript fasting-days, the doctrine that is not evidently determined by scripture, ought to stand free and indifferent. But the doctrine of the necessity of company to receive with the priest is nowhere determined so by the scripture: it should stand then by your vain principle as free, and a thing indifferent. And will you have freedom in scripture driven to necessity without scripture? Will you clog us with the very tittle and syllable of the scripture, and suck out a bond of necessity from thence to enforce us to do in all points the like, and specially in the order of the ministration of the holy sacrament of the altar? Then must we ask you, how dare you minister the sacrament in England, seeing that Christ only ministered it in Jewry? And here you must confess the observation of the place precisely not to be necessary. Why minister you unto women, when Christ ministered it unto men? Here you will grant that

CAP. VI.

A.

B.

you are not constrained by God's law unto the male. Why do you minister it in the morning before dinner, when Christ ministered it in the evening after supper? True it is, you will say, that Christ ministered it after supper, but he gave no law to bind unto that time. Why enterprize you to do that upon Sundays often, that Christ did once upon Shere-Thursday? You will answer in like wise, that there is no scripture that commandeth us to forbear any day in the year. Why do you that openly in the church, that Christ did secretly in a parlour? Because we have no commandment in scripture to forbear any property of place. Why do you minister it to the laity, where Christ gave it only unto the apostles that were priests? You will say, that we have no commandment to exclude any state of men. Why do you minister it to more or fewer, when Christ ministered it only unto twelve? And what answer have you here, but to say as you said before, that as place, sex, time, day, degree, state of people, secretness, are nothing appertaining as necessary to the substance of the sacrament; so number is but an accident or an ornament rather to beautify the devotion of christian people in receiving the sacrament, than thereunto appertaining as necessary unto the substance? And thus may you perceive, that when you require the like doing to Christ herein in every small point or tittle in us, as in place, time, sex, day, state of people, secretness, number, you deceive yourselves, and others. Taking these things to be necessary for the safeguard of

OF PRIVATE MASS. 19

the substance of the sacrament, the which are nothing else but very accidents: the alteration whereof do lie in the discretion of spiritual governors, without damage or hurt done to the substance of the sacrament or the use thereof: and are to be counted amongst such things, as St Paul speaketh of, when he wrote, *Cetera cum venero disponam;* "I will set the other things in order, when I come." [1 Cor. xi.34.]

But the great matter you harp on, to have company together in one place to receive at any time with the priest, is because that in the use of this sacrament there ought to be a communion. And I pray you, is not there a communion among all Christians in prayer? For in our prayer we say, our Father, not my Father, which art in heaven; thy will be done in earth, as it is in heaven; not in me, as it is in heaven; give us this day our daily bread; we say not, give me this day my daily bread; forgive us our trespasses; we say not, forgive me my trespasses, &c. Whereby we know that we communicate in prayer with all Christendom, being members of one mystical body of Christ. And will you inhibit me to say my *Pater noster* when I am alone in my chamber, void of company to say with me, or will you shut up all Christendom in some narrow room, that they may be together at one time to say the Lord's prayer? Or will you grant that there may be a communion in prayer amongst all Christians, without any respect to have them together at one time in any one place, and that there can

CAP. VII.

A.

B. be no communion in the use of the sacrament, unless all the communicants be together in one place, and at one time? Have you any scripture to lead you to say, that the communion in the use of the sacrament must of necessity have all the communicants in one place at one time close up, more than the communion in prayer? One of the articles of the Creed is, *Credo sanctorum communionem.* "I believe the communion of saints." I believe we have communion in baptism, in penance, in confirmation, in extreme unction, in prayer, in fasting, in almsdeeds. And must all they that practise any of these, be driven to do it at one place, in one season, or else to have no part of such a communion as there is comprised in these holy sacraments? Is this your doctrine? Where have you these in scripture? There is an old doctor, called Dionysius, that teacheth us why it is called a communion[1]: not because it requireth unity and identity of time and place in the communicants; but because all Christians thereby, being lively members of one body first, are brought to an unity with Christ their head, and then every member with the mystical body; and then every member with other. So that in the working of this marvellous unity, number, time, and place are no principal doers, but foreigners and very strangers in-

[1 Ἑκάστης ἱεροτελεστικῆς πραγματείας καὶ τὰς μεριστὰς ἡμῶν ζωὰς εἰς ἑνοειδῆ θέωσιν συναγούσης, καὶ τῇ τῶν διαιρετῶν θεοειδεῖ συμπτύξει τὴν πρὸς τὸ ἓν κοινωνίαν καὶ ἕνωσιν δωρουμένης.—DIONYS. AREOP. De Eccles. Hierarch. c. 3. Op. ed. Antwerp. 1634. Tom. I. p. 282.]

deed. And the place of St Paul meaneth no less in the first to the Corinthians: *Quo-* [1 Cor. x. 17.] *niam unus panis et unum corpus multi sumus, omnes quidem de uno pane et de uno calice participamus:* whereby we hear that Christians are partakers of one loaf; and yet there is no one particular place able to receive them, nor yet no one particular loaf able to serve them.

Surely as touching your fancy to have of necessity the communicants closed up in one place, there to be served at one especial time, or else to be no partakers of the communion,   c. it will fall in process of reasoning to so many follies; that we must know how large the place must be, and how long you will appoint the time appertaining to one communion. And as for the place, when the multitude of the communicants are very great, whether may be a communion betwixt him that receiveth at the altar in our lady chapel in Paul's, and him that receiveth in the lowest place of the west end of Paul's church? If there may, why are they not partakers of one communion that receive in two divers churches in London, not so far distant the one from the other, as our lady chapel is from the west end of Paul's? And if they cannot, let us know why; and have some scripture for proof thereof. If they may, why may not the communicants be partakers of one communion in three churches; and why not be partakers of one communion in four or five churches no further distant? If not, limit you then the furthest distance that a communion may be had in, and bring in scriptures, doctors, or any councils to prove the limitation, and we will cry creake[1]. And in like manner we may reason for the appointment of time. Appoint you the longest time that a communion may be had, and shew some good evidence for your limitation. And likewise we will cry creake. You drive men to these trifles that the world may know you hang in nifels[2].

CAP. VIII.
A.

Erasmus Roterodamus, in his epistle that he wrote against false gospellers, reporteth how they were wont in the old time in the primitive church, to deliver every one the sacrament in their hands to bear home with them and receive it when their devotion served. *Olim* (saith he) *corpus domini dabatur in manu, ut domi, cum vellent, sumerent qui accepissent*[3]. "The Lord's body in old time was delivered into folks' hands, to the intent that they who had taken it might receive it when they would." When divers people took the Lord's body in their hands to receive it at home in their several houses when their devotion served them to receive it, are any yet so unwise to think, that they that so received it, were either in one place, considering their houses were several, or at any one time, considering the variety of their devotions, wills, purposes, and trade of life? Do you not see in these few words, that the partakers of

[1 *Crie creake*, i. e. *confess that we are in error*.]
[2 *Nifels*, i. e. *things of naught*.]
[3 DESID. ERASMI Epist. in Pseudevangelicos. Op. ed. Lug. Bat. 1706. Tom. x. col. 1585. But for *manu* read *manum*.]

any one communion were not wont to be clogged to receive it in any place or at any one especial time? Do not you manifestly hear a reservation of the sacrament confessed here? And whereas it was delivered in their hands, as wine is not, understand you not thereby a communion under one kind? But you will say it was but Erasmus' report; but I say he reported it as he found in ancient writers. And Erasmus, pardie, was wont to be a great man amongst you: and do you so little esteem him now? You have overrun him (I grant), as you have done Luther, that was once your God.

Erasmus is not the first father of this report. But Tertullian himself, which flourished not long after the apostles' time, in his second book that he wrote to his wife, reporteth no less. How that the christian wife kept it close from her husband, being a Paynim, that she received every morning secretly before meat. And if it so happed that he espied it, that he would think it were bread: and not that which christian men took it to be. *Non sciet maritus quid secreto ante omnem cibum gustes. Et si sciverit, panem non illum credit esse qui dicitur*[1]. "Thy husband shall not know what thou dost eat secretly before thy meat. And if he do know it, he believeth that it is bread, and not he whom we call it." Ponder these words well, and see whether it agreeth not with Erasmus' report. When the christian wife did secretly receive the holy sacrament, was there any company re-

B.

[1 TERTULL. Ad uxorem, Lib. II. c. 5.]

ceived with her? Can a thing done in company, be secret? Or could she keep close from the Paynim, her husband, that thing that should be often practised in any open assembly? Were not, think you, the Paynims, that at that time were the greater number, diligent to search what the Christians did? Seemeth it not in her secret receiving before all meats, that she reserved the sacrament at home, to receive it when she would? And where Tertullian saith, that if it chanced that her husband knew what she eat, he would think it to be bread, (making no mention, he would think it to be wine) and not the very body of Christ, as the Christians do confess. Furthermore, seemeth not this woman to have received it under one kind? For her husband that saw her eat the form of bread, that was wont to be first received, would soon have perceived when she drank the form of wine, that should be immediately received after. To conclude, it appeareth by these old writers, that this woman received alone, without any company to receive with her. And that she reserved the sacrament with her at home, to receive at her own house when she list. And last of all, that she received under one kind.

St Cyprian also, the great clerk and glorious martyr, touching the reservation of the holy sacrament, in the first sermon *De Lapsis*, telleth of a woman which reserved the sacrament in her coffer at home, that went about unreverently to open the coffer: how a fire rose up from thence, and so feared her, that she durst not to touch it.

His words be these: *Cum quædam arcam suam, in qua domini sanctum fuit, manibus indignis tentasset aperire, igne inde surgente deterrita est ne auderet attingere*[1]. "When a certain woman (saith he) unworthily essayed to open her own coffer, wherein the holy body of our Lord was, a fire rose thence, and feared her that she durst not touch it at all." See you not yet where Erasmus learned that the lay-people took the sacrament in their hands and reserved it at home, to receive it reverently when their devotion served? Hath not Tertullian reported the same? Doth not St Cyprian in the former words import the same? The woman had the sacrament in her coffer at home: and will you deny the reservation? She came unreverently to open the coffer, and to receive the sacrament, being alone: and will you suppress the sole receiving? The fire rose up from thence, and for fear she touched it not: would God have wrought this miracle, if the sacrament had been nothing else but common bread when it was reserved?

Cyril, that ancient father, saith, that it is not only folly to deny the reservation, but a very madness indeed. He writeth to Calosirius, that they are mad that say, the body of Christ remaineth not in such portions consecrated, as are kept to the next day after the consecration. *Insaniunt igitur dicentes* (saith he) *mysticam benedictionem a sanctificatione cessare, si quæ reliquiæ ejus*

[1 CYPR. De Lapsis. Op. ed. Fell. Oxon. 1682. P. I. p. 132, 3.]

D.

remanserint in sequentem diem. Non enim mutabitur sacrosanctum corpus Christi, sed virtus, benedictio et vivificativa gratia magis in eo est[1]. "They are then mad that say, the mystical benediction or blessing leaveth from the sanctification, if any leaving remain of it till the next day. For the very holy body of Christ shall not be changed. But the power and virtue and the lively quickening grace is continually abiding in it without company to receive."

When ye hear Chrysostom tell of the daily sacrifice; when you hear the ancient father, Cyrillus, call them mad that deny the reservation; when ye hear him say plainly and flatly, that there is no alteration in the very holy body of Christ, though it be kept, and the virtue, and full power of the consecration, and the lively quickening grace doth continue still in the holy portions that are reserved; when St Cyprian, that holy martyr, maketh report of the holy sacrament reserved at home in the woman's coffer, to receive when her lust, when devotion served her: and when he sheweth that God wrought the miracle in the stirring of the fire from it, because she thought to use it unreverently, to cause her to forbear; when Tertullian afore that agreeth with the same; and when Erasmus

[[1] Ἀκούω δὲ ὅτι εἰς ἁγιασμὸν ἀπρακτεῖν φασὶν τὴν μυστικὴν εὐλογίαν, εἰ ἀπομένοι λείψανον αὐτῆς εἰς ἑτέραν ἡμέραν. Μαίνονται δὲ ταῦτα λέγοντες· οὐ γὰρ ἀλλοιοῦται Χριστός, οὐδὲ τὸ ἅγιον αὐτοῦ σῶμα μεταβληθήσεται, ἀλλ' ἡ τῆς εὐλογίας δύναμις καὶ ἡ ζωοποιὸς χάρις διηνεκής ἐστιν ἐν αὐτῷ.—CYRILL. ALEX. Epist. ad Calosyrium præfix. libro Advers. Anthropomorphitas. Op. ed. Auberti. Lutet. 1638. Tom. vi. p. 365.]

Roterodamus, a man famous in his time, recordeth the matter as he had learned it of these holy fathers and other: that the people received it in their hands, received it at home, received it when every man saw his time: Shall any man continue so impudent to deny that ever people used the sole receiving without company, or deny the reservation? The scripture saith, *In ore duorum vel trium, &c.* Two or three witnesses are able to try any matter: and especially such witnesses as these are, men of holy life, ancient fathers of great learning, called forth to witness the truth from every quarter of the world, some from Asia, some from Africa, some from Europa, &c.

What say you to Satyrus, that hanged the holy sacrament about his neck in a stole, when he went to the sea? What say you to the great clerk, St Ambrose, bishop of Milan, that praised him greatly for his so doing[1]? Appeared not there a reservation? And I trow, under one kind, unless your brain will

E.

[1 Quid igitur observantiam ejus erga Dei cultum prædicem? Qui priusquam perfectioribus esset initiatus mysteriis, in naufragio constitutus, cum ea qua veheretur navis, scopuloso illisa vado, et urgentibus hinc atque inde fluctibus solveretur, non mortem metuens, sed ne vacuus mysterii exiret e vita, quos initiatos esse cognoverat, ab his divinum illud fidelium sacramentum poposcit: non ut curiosos oculos inferret arcanis, sed ut fidei suæ consequeretur auxilium. Etenim ligari fecit in orario, et orarium involvit collo, atque ita se dejecit in mare, non requirens de navis compage resolutam tabulam, cui supernatans juvaretur, quoniam fidei solius arma quæsierat. Itaque his se tectum atque munitum satis credens, alia auxilia non desideravit.—AMBROS. De excessu fratris sui Satyri. Lib. I. § 43. Op. ed. Bened. Paris. Tom. II. col. 1125.]

serve you to enclose wine in a stole, as mine will not.

CAP. IX.

What say you by Syrapion, who, being in despair of his life, sent for the priest to minister him the sacrament in the night season. But when the priest lay sick in his bed, and could not go himself, he took Syrapion's lad the sacrament in his hand, and bade him moist it, and so minister it into the mouth of his sick master. The priest was sick and could not rise. The lad came in the night time, the priest delivered the sacrament into his hand, he bade him moist it, and give it to the sick[1]. And

A.

doth not this prove, both that the priest had reserved it, and the moisting thereof that the sick man took it under one kind, and when he sent no more than would serve the sick man, was not there the houselling of one alone without company?

The twelfth canon of Nicene council provideth for such as are like to depart this life, to receive the sacrament or they depart. And if any such that is in that case houselled, chance to recover, then to be amongst the

[[1] The narrative is given by Dionysius, bishop of Alexandria, in a letter to Fabius, bishop of Antioch, and preserved from thence by Eusebius in his Ecclesiastical History, Bk. VI. c. 44. The words upon which our author's argument depends, and which are criticized below in the "Answer," are these:—Βραχὺ τῆς εὐχαριστίας ἐπέδωκεν τῷ παιδαρίῳ, ἀποβρέξαι κελεύσας· καὶ τῷ πρέσβυτῃ κατὰ τοῦ στόματος ἐπιστάξαι. And on his return:—ἀπέβρεξεν ὁ παῖς, καὶ ἅμα τε ἐνέχεε τῷ στόματι· καὶ μικρὸν ἐκεῖνος καταβροχθίσας εὐθέως ἀπέδωκε τὸ πνεῦμα.—Euseb. Hist. Eccl. Lib. VI. c. 44. ed. Reading. Cant. 1720. Tom. I. p. 317, 318.]

communicants' prayer. The words be these: *De iis qui recedunt ex corpore, antiqua legis regula observabitur etiam nunc. Ita ut si quis forte recedat ex corpore, necessario vitæ suæ viatico non defraudetur. Quod si desperatus aliquis recepta communione supervixerit, sit inter eos qui sola oratione communicant*[1]. "Concerning those that depart this life, the old rule of the law shall be kept now also. So that any be like to depart this life, he be not deceived of his necessary voyage-provision for his life. If he that was in despair of life, after that he received the communion chance to recover, let him be amongst them that do communicate by prayers only." The holy ancient council of all the learned fathers at Nice, thought it convenient that such as were like to die, should be houselled before their departing: and could this rule be inviolably kept amongst so many casualties of sickness and sudden infections and divers other chances that fall at divers and sundry times, both by day and night, unless the holy sacrament were reserved? And unless every man received as necessity served alone without company, when necessity so required? Sometime the priest, as Chrysostom saith, in the celebration of the daily sacrifice receiveth without the people : and sometime

B.

[[1] Περὶ τῶν ἐξοδευόντων ὁ παλαιὸς καὶ κανονικὸς νόμος φυλαχθήσεται καὶ νῦν, ὥστε εἴ τις ἐξοδεύοι, τοῦ δεσποτικοῦ ἐφοδίου μὴ ἀποστερείσθω· εἰ δὲ ἀπογνωσθεὶς καὶ κοινωνίας τυχὼν, καὶ προσφορᾶς μετασχὼν, πάλιν ἐν τοῖς ζῶσιν ἐξετασθείη, ἔστω μετὰ τῶν κοινωνούντων τῆς εὐχῆς μόνης.— SYNOD. NIC. Can. 13. Apud Gelasii Cyzic. Comm. Act. Nic. Concil. ed. Commelin. 1604. fol. p. 46.]

the people without the priest: and sometime one alone without any company at all, as we have at large shewed afore.

CAP. X.

In the bishop's and priest's absence, the deacons received alone, if they were disposed to receive; as the fourteenth canon of the ancient and old council of Nice hath taken order. The words be these: *Pervenit ad sanctum concilium, quod in locis quibusdam et civitatibus presbyteris diaconi sacramenta porrigant. Hoc neque regula, neque consuetudo tradit, ut ii, qui offerendi sacrificii potestatem non habent, hiis qui offerunt corpus Christi porrigant. Sed et illud innotuit, quod quidam diaconi etiam ante episcopum sacramenta sumant. Hæc ergo omnia amputentur, et accipiant secundum ordinem post presbyteros ab episcopo, vel a presbytero, sacram communionem. Quod si non fuerit in presenti vel episcopus, vel presbyter, tunc ipsi proferant et edant*[1]. "It is reported to

[1 The translation of this canon by Dionysius Exiguus, as given by Hardouin, stands thus:—Pervenit ad sanctum concilium, quod, in locis quibusdam et civitatibus, presbyteris sacramenta diaconi porrigant. Hoc neque regula, neque consuetudo tradidit: ut hi qui offerendi sacrificii non habent potestatem, his qui offerunt, corpus Christi porrigant. Sed et illud innotuit, quod quidam diacones etiam ante episcopos sacramenta sumunt. Hæc ergo omnia amputentur, et maneant diacones intra suam propriam mensuram: scientes quia episcoporum quidem ministri sunt, presbyteris autem inferiores. Accipiant ergo secundum ordinem post presbyteros ab episcopo, vel a presbytero, sacram communionem. Quod si non fuerit in præsenti vel episcopus, vel presbyter, tunc ipsi proferant et edant. Sed nec sedere quidem licet in medio presbyterorum diacones: extra regulam enim est, ut hoc fiat. Si quis autem non vult

the holy council, that in certain places and cities the deacons deliver the sacrament to the priests. Neither rule, neither custom, taught this, that they that have no authority to offer sacrifice should deliver the body of Christ to them that offer it. And another thing also came to our ears, that there are certain deacons who receive the sacrament before the bishop. Wherefore let all such things be cut off, let them receive the holy communion, orderly, after the priests, of the bishops or priest. And if the bishop or the priest be absent, let themselves bring it forth and eat it." If the deacons, as it appeareth by this canon, that had no authority to consecrate, and to offer the sacrifice of Christ's body and blood, might, in the bishop's or priest's absence, fetch forth the

his sufficiens esse post hanc definitionem, cesset esse diaconus.—Hard. Concil. Tom. I. p. 329, 30. The Greek, as given by Gelasius Cyzicenus, (which is almost identical with that of Hardouin) stands thus: —Ἦλθεν εἰς τὴν ἁγίαν καὶ μεγάλην Σύνοδον, ὅτι ἔν τισι τόποις ἢ πόλεσι πρεσβυτέροις τὴν εὐχαριστίαν οἱ Διάκονοι διδόασιν, ὅπερ οὔτε ὁ κανὼν οὔτε ἡ συνήθεια παρέδωκε, τοὺς ἐξουσίαν μὴ ἔχοντας προσφέρειν, τούτους τοῖς προσφέρουσι διδόναι τὸ σῶμα τοῦ Χριστοῦ. Κἀκεῖνο δὲ ἐγνωρίσθη, ὅτι ἤδη τινὲς τῶν Διακόνων καὶ πρὸ τῶν ἐπισκόπων τῆς εὐχαριστίας ἅπτονται. Ταῦτα οὖν πάντα περιηρείσθω· καὶ ἐμμενέτωσαν οἱ Διάκονοι τοῖς ἰδίοις μέτροις, εἰδότες ὅτι τοῦ μὲν ἐπισκόπου ὑπηρέται εἰσί, τῶν δὲ πρεσβυτέρων ἐλάττους τυγχάνουσι. Λαμβανέτωσαν δὲ κατὰ τάξιν τὴν εὐχαριστίαν μετὰ τοὺς πρεσβυτέρους, ἢ τοῦ ἐπισκόπου αὐτοῖς διδόντος ἢ τοῦ πρεσβυτέρου. Ἀλλὰ μήτε καθῆσθαι ἐν μέσῳ τῶν πρεσβυτέρων ἐξέστω τοῖς Διακόνοις· παρὰ κανόνα γὰρ καὶ παρὰ τάξιν ἐστὶ τὸ γινόμενον. Εἰ δέ τις μὴ θέλοι πειθαρχεῖν, καὶ μετὰ τοὺς ὅρους πεπαύσθω τῆς Διακονίας.— Can. 18. Gelas. Cyzic. Conc. Nic. ed. 1604. p. 47.]

sacrament, and receive it, can you deny but it was reserved? And that the same grace of Christ's body remained in the holy sacrament after the consecration in the bishop's and priest's absence? Which could by no means be consecrated, but by the bishop's and priest's presence. I will not cavil with you upon the term above rehearsed in the canon, concerning the deacons, that they might, in the bishop's and priest's absence, bring forth the sacrament and eat it: which is proper to the form of bread and not to the form of wine: and thereby declare that the deacons received it but in one kind. Notwithstanding I might as well stand therein, and better too, than you stand upon *Accipite et manducate*, and *bibite ex hoc omnes*, to drive the sacrament immediately without any reservation to his use, and that at every communion there must of necessity be a company to receive with the priest, and every one of the lay people ought of necessity to receive the same in both kinds. I will not, I say, use no such dalliance upon the word, 'eat,' in the canon, as you use in, "take eat and drink all of this" in the use of the sacrament very sophistically. But let go all such vantage upon tittles. I am contented to use none other proof but such as all men that have any discretion do so evidently perceive to be so good, that they are never able to find any occasion in the world to control it. Such as I have used before, for the proof of private mass, reservation, the sole receiving, or ministration of the sacrament in certain cases under one kind, to have been used in the state of the primitive church.

Read St Cyprian in his fifth sermon, *De lapsis:* there shall you see that the deacon gave an infant, that had received before part of such meats as were sacrificed up to the idols, a portion of Christ's blood out of the chalice. And as soon as the infant received it, it was wonderfully vexed, because it was marvellous dishonour to the blood of Christ to be poured into the mouth that was a little before defiled with the idol's sacrifice. And thereby may you understand, that the infant received the sacrament of the deacon under the form of wine only, and not under the form of bread. For by that reason, if the infant had received it under the form of bread before, being part of the sacrament as precious as the other, it should have been vexed very sore before the cup had been offered it. But the first vexation that it had was, when the deacon gave the sacrament in form of wine. And therefore it is evident, that the deacon gave not the infant the sacrament under the form of bread[1]. And was not this a communion

CAP. XI.

[[1] Cyprian's account of the matter (to which attention is directed below in the "Answer") is this:—
Puella mixta cum sanctis, precis nostræ et orationis impatiens, nunc ploratu concuti, nunc mentis æstu cœpit fluctuabunda jactari, et velut tortore cogente, quibus poterat indiciis conscientiam facti in simplicibus adhuc annis rudis anima fatebatur. Ubi vero solennibus adimpletis calicem diaconus offerre præsentibus cœpit, et accipientibus ceteris locus ejus advenit, faciem suam parvula instinctu divinæ majestatis avertere, os labiis obturantibus premere,

under one kind only? You have heard now, I suppose, not a word, or half word, not one sentence, or half a sentence, as your calling was, but many, and full proofs against certain of your assertions. And by these you have good cause to distrust all the rest of your doctrine.

CHAP. XII.

A.

Thus far my leisure served me, being otherwise occupied with business enough, to answer in the defence of my spiritual mother, the catholic church. Not for because it was our part, that are in possession, to render any reason for our right, wherein prescription of time out of mind is a sufficient bar: but partly, because I saw your importunity in calling upon them to strike, that you had bound in recognisance of great sums to be forfeited, if they had gone about to give you any blow. So that you may perceive well by this, that they are better armed than you thought they were: when I, who am nothing in comparison of the learned doctors of this realm, being a man of no great reading, but in stories, am yet able thus to say in so good a matter, that I trust you will hereafter leave your importunity of provoking so many learned men of this realm, to shew what evidence they have for the truth. It had been more rea-

calicem recusare. Perstitit tamen diaconus, et reluctanti licet, de sacramento calicis infudit. Tunc sequitur singultus et vomitus. In corpore atque ore violato Eucharistia permanere non potuit. Sanctificatus in Domini sanguine potus de pollutis visceribus erupit; tanta est potestas Domini, tanta majestas.— CYPR. De Lapsis. Op. ed. Fell. Ox. 1682, P. 1. p. 132.]

sonable, that you (that would dispossess us of the interest we have in the true doctrine, that the catholic church first taught us, and hath recorded sufficiently in her practice these fifteen hundred years and more, and in records of writers this nine hundred years and sixty, as yourself do seem to confess) should shew sufficient causes, why we ought to be dispossessed, rather than we to lay for ourselves proofs to keep possession. I marvel that you think it not hurt to your side, to grant that the whole practice of the church hath run with us this nine hundred years and threescore: whereas, in possession of lands, quiet possession for the space of one hundred years or two, putteth the case out of all doubt.

You hang upon the state of the six hundred years, that were next after Christ, and you see how that the whole record of the state runneth against you. Tertullian is against you; Cyprian is against you; Eusebius is against you; Ambrose is against you; Cyril is against you; the holy and ancient council of Nice is against you. And yet you will make the people to ween, that all are with you of that state. I have not brought in the empty names, as apothecaries do upon their boxes, but have shewed you what good drugs they have. I have not cast out from the wall any victuals in your assault, to make a brag in penury, as many of your part commonly use to do, as though they had great plenty of victuals; but have brought you unto the sight of such provision, as the holy ancient fathers of the primitive church,

B.

C.

such as yourselves do allow, have made for us. But come unto the practice of the church, and records of the fathers, of the latter nine hundred years: they cry so thick and threefold against you, that you are not able to abide them. And therefore you were wont to disgrace them all. By what authority, I pray you, would you have them all discredited? It savoureth of a marvellous arrogancy, to discredit them all. Can your doctrine creep no other ways into credit, unless you deface the practices of the church, and the authority of the fathers, for the space of nine hundred years and odd? Have you no other means to get honour, but to dishonour so many ancient fathers, as have written this latter nine hundred years? Know you not the scripture, *Qui maledixerit patri vel matri morte morietur?* And what malediction is there greater, than to blaze that our learned fathers (that lived so godly in prayers, fastings, almsdeeds, continual study of doctrine, that hath their common agreements for the space of nine hundred years and more) deceived Christ's flock, knew not the right faith, but trained the people to the state of damnation?

And, I pray you, if they were so many years deceived, and yet given all the while to spiritual exercises more than you, as it appeareth by their works, or any now-a-days, what assurance can you make us, that you do now know the truth? Being a man far underneath them in all points; and one that hath not continued here much (as I hear say) above forty years, and not bestowed the fourth part of that time neither (as I hear) in study of the scriptures or old doctors? Shall you, with nine or ten years' study in the matters of doctrine, think yourself able to sit as a judge, to control all such doctors, and the doctrine which they have left in record for the space of nine hundred years? No man gave you such authority but yourself. Luther and Melancthon took upon them to be reformers of religion in all points. But if you mark them, they make no matter of necessity to communicate the laity with both kinds. They acknowledge that a general council may take order in it, as a thing indifferent, and having no scripture for the proof of the necessity thereof. They confirm also the being of Christ's body in a thousand places at once, meaning therein as the catholics mean.

If you had acquainted yourself with Abraham and Isaac, (that said[1] that *quæcunque promisit Deus, potens est et facere;* "whatsoever God promiseth, he is able to perform it;") or with the angel, (that said unto Mary in as great a matter as this is, *Non est impossibile apud Deum omne verbum;* "There is no word impossible unto God;") as well as you have acquainted yourself with Ismael and Agar, that see no farther than the trade of common nature; or if you had marked but the very rule of nature, how of an antecedent granted all necessary consequence[s] do by force of reason issue there hence, you would never put the

[1 That is, Abraham with reference to Isaac.]

CAP. XIII.

[Rom. iv. 21.]

[Luke i. 37.]

matter in question. We find in scripture that our Saviour said, in the consecration [Luke xxii. 19.] of the blessed sacrament, *This is my body, that shall be delivered for you.* And when the sense of this sentence is, as the catholic church teacheth, the very real presence of Christ's body to be in the blessed sacrament, upon this sense, once settled, many labels do necessarily hang; not expressedly had in scripture, but by drift of reason out of the first verity gathered. And so did St Chrysostome, St Ambrose, St Basil, and St Bernard, when they understood the sense of Christ's words concerning the consecration to be as the holy catholic church understood it: and not to have power in the parlour at Jerusalem only, where the sacrament was first instituted, but in all places, where the thing was so practised as Christ began it. Thereunto they saw they must needs confess by drift of argument, that Christ's body is in divers places at once: and of the remainders of the accidents, you need no other proof, but your own senses, your eye, and your tasting. And of the alteration of the substance of bread, the fathers in divers ages saw it so depend upon the first verity, that they have omitted no variety of terms, to express it and to bring it into the knowledge of the world. They have *transmutation, transelementation, mutation, conversion, faction, alteration, transubstantiation*, and divers other such, that are not to be rehearsed now. You have taken upon you to control the council of Constance already: but now you will control the great council of Lateran, where were so many learned clerks as there were never more gathered together; and the council of Valence, and the council of Rome, *sub Nicolao*, and the general council of Florence, and the council of Basil[1]: in the which all your errors, concerning the holy sacrament, are overthrown.

Concerning your doubt how Christ's body is in divers places at once, sithen you believe no council that hath determined that matter, nor ancient fathers, Greeks nor Latins, I will send you to your great god, Luther, in a little book that he wrote against the Zwinglians, of the sense of the words of the supper of Christ. They yet remain undefaced. There he answereth you at the full. Or else to Brentius, that great Cain, in the exposition of the article of the ascension in the first of the Acts, where he interpreteth thereof at the full, though very far in divers points from the sense of the church. Yet may he not suffer that blind reason of yours to have his force in no case. It is but a very fond dalliance to brawl upon the labels before you agree upon the original verity. The true sense of this little sentence, *This is my body that shall be delivered for you*, is the root and the original of all such labels as we teach, not mentioned in scripture expressly, but boulted out by drift of argument, as these are, that offend you so sore.

When the master saith to his servant, Make

A similitude for unwritten verities.

[1 Council of Constance, a. 1414 to 1418. Lateran, a. 1215. Valence, a. 1248. Rome, under Nicolas II., a. 1059. Florence, a. 1439. Basil, a. 1431 to 1443.]

ready that I may dine; he speaketh nothing in these words of scumming of the pot, of clean water for the potage, of the herbs to be chopped, of scalding and drawing the capons, of making a fire, of hewing of wood, of laying the cloth, and other things necessary belonging to his dinner. And yet, if the servant would leave the pot unscummed, herbs ungathered, make potage with stinking water, put the capon upon the broche, feathers, guts and all, because his master made no express mention of the particular ordering of all these: I ween no man would allow his wit or honesty. Because in his master's first commandment all such necessaries are implied. And so we answer you as your mother the catholic church hath taught us. We need not to shew you of accidents, remaining without any subject, nor of Christ's body being in divers places at once, nor of the adoration of the holy sacrament, nor of many other trifling doubts you make: because all such doubts are answered to the full, in the original verity of Christ's words, being in the nature of the verity necessarily implied. As these are, against the which you may kick, till you be weary: but it lieth not in you to alter the nature of Christ's own words.

If you had found in the scripture, spoken by Christ concerning the blessed sacrament, *This is not my body, but the figure of my body, being absent in substance, and only present to your imaginations, by the sight of the bread;* you might have triumphed and blowed up your horn lustily in every pulpit, and made your avaunt, that you had been able to control all Christendom. But now the letter is very plain against you, and the sense of the letter also, as the fathers do record in all ages, and general councils too: as may appear by your own mistrust for the space of the last nine hundred years and odd.

I take God to judge, I wrote not this for any malice to such as are otherwise bent. I pity them rather, and daily pray for them, that they may embrace the catholic faith. But when I perceived Golias in his bravery, having trust in his big bones and strong weapons, bragging many times, as though there were none of the Israelites able to match him: notwithstanding there are very many that could have handled him better than I, being a man of small learning, troubled with much business; yet I thought it my duty, for the honour of my mother, the catholic church, to hurl out four or five stones in David's sling against this champion: not to hurt him in the forehead, as David did Golias, but to crush in pieces certain untruths that he taught; wishing him as well to do as I would myself; and all my countrymen of England to beware, lest they fall into the snares and traps that our ghostly enemy layeth abroad everywhere, not only to hurt their bodies, but to hurl down both body and soul into the deep dungeon of hell. The which I beseech God most heartily give all men grace to avoid. Amen.

An Answere in
Defence of the truth.
Against the
Apologie
of
Private
Masse.

LONDINI.
Mens. Nouëb.
1562.

[The above title is in a compartment with Lucretia in a medallion at the bottom.]

THE CHIEF POINTS TOUCHED IN THIS DEFENCE OF THE TRUTH.

Against private mass, or sole receiving by the minister, in the common place of prayer.

Why the doctors call the sacrament of the Lord's supper by the name of oblation or sacrifice.

Against communion under one kind.

Of reservation of the sacrament.

Against the arguments of multitude and long continuance of time.

Against the alleging of the authority and name of the church.

What is to be attributed to the ancient fathers.

Of real presence and interpretation of Christ's words, *Hoc est corpus*, &c.

THE PREFACE

TO

THE READER.

It is well known to a great number, partly by presence in hearing, partly by writing set forth of the same, that a worthy learned man and bishop of this realm[1], stoutly indeed, as the matter required, and clerkly also, as learning and knowledge taught him, did openly protest in certain sermons, not to the furtherance of untruth, as malice carpeth, but to the confusion of falsehood, as the end proveth; that, if any of those things which he then rehearsed, could be proved of the contrary side by any sufficient authority of the scriptures, old doctors, and ancient councils, or by any allowed example of the primitive church, then he would be contented to subscribe and yield to their doctrine. This his doing, as no less was to be looked for, some men depraved, many dispraised, all they misliked, that maintained such superstitious errors, as false teaching hath trained people in, the space of certain hundred years. And indeed, seeing they heard their doctrine so plainly defaced, and their wilful misleading of christian men so openly to be noted, a man may think they had good cause to startle at the matter, and somewhat to look about them, lest they

[1 John Jewel, Bishop of Salisbury.]

seemed altogether careless. Wherefore, as divers have diversly shewed their misliking, so one of that party hath in writing privily spread abroad an answer to the foresaid offer or protestation for private masses: wherein he both persuadeth himself, and would have other also to believe, that he hath so fully satisfied the party's request, as it may seem great folly, and as he termeth it, impudency, any longer to stay upon it. One of the copies of this answer by occasion, as it fortuned, not many months since, lighted into my hands: which, I understand, is so spread abroad in divers places of this realm, as there be few mislikers of the truth, but they have it, and make such account of it, as a great number of the unlearned sort stay their consciences thereupon.

Who the author is, or what manner of man, I neither know, nor can guess more, than he witnesseth of himself in the entrance of this treatise; where he signifieth, that once he embraced that religion, which he now detesteth and writeth against. In that part methinketh he doth deal, as fond men sometime are wont to do; which, to displease their enemies, stick not to hurt themselves also. So he, to discredit the doctrine that he is revolted from, giveth such testimony of his own naughty life and conscience, as he would be loth to hear at any man's mouth but his own. "All that time," saith he, "I neither regarded God, nor good religion, nor any good conscience beside." What malice it is to charge the doctrine, that by hypocrisy he professed, with the cause of his evil doing, I will not declare with such words as the matter requireth. This much I will say, that he learned this of old Adam's great counsellor: who, at the beginning, being blamed for his disobedience, seemed to burden God himself with the cause of it, and excused his own folly by that thing, which his Maker had given him to his comfort and commodity. In like manner, when this man's conscience, as it seemeth by his own words, accused him of lewd living and lack of the fear of God, to excuse his own ill disposed mind, he casteth the fault upon the doctrine of the gospel, which God did open unto him undoubtedly to his great commodity, if he would have taken it. And under this pretence, both forsaketh it himself, and by his example exhorteth other to eschew it. But as the wicked life of a man, to his own great harm, may be a blot to the religion that he professeth: so God forbid it should be counted a full reproof of the same, or a just cause to be of all other rejected. If it were so, men should refuse Christianity, because divers, not of the basest sort, but of the heads of the church, as their own histories witness, have been of horrible and wicked life. But we must think, that the hypocrisy and traitorous covetousness of Judas and his fellows is a confusion to themselves, but no just reproach to Christ that they follow, or to his doctrine that they seem to profess. I will judge and hope better of this writer, to whom with all my heart I wish much more good; trusting that God shall once again open his heart to receive the truth, which I cannot but think God hath taken from him in punishment of that naughty conscience, that he witnesseth hath been in himself. But, whatsoever he be, let him stand or fall to his Lord God. I will not take upon me to judge him, neither would I have spoken this much of him, but that he doth odiously excuse his own evil mind by the good doctrine of Christ's gospel. My purpose is to confute his doctrine, I will not meddle with his person. I intend to answer his cavilling at other men's words and doings: I mind not to discredit or deface his estimation or honesty.

And yet in this point I know some may judge me presumptuous and arrogant, that I seem to take upon me his quarrel, who is far better able to answer for himself than I am. But I would desire those which so think, to consider; first, that this is a common quarrel, touching not only him that is named, but all other that either teacheth or believeth as he doth : secondly, that he against whom this writing is directed, either knoweth not that any such thing is spread, or, if he do know it, either thinketh it not worthy answer of itself, or else hath not at this present such leisure as he may intend to answer it: thirdly and chiefly, that by private conference with certain persons I understand, perhaps more than either he or any other doth think, how much this treatise is esteemed among many, which otherwise happily might be persuaded to embrace the gospel. Therefore I have been moved the sooner myself, in such sort as I might, to shape an answer unto it. For to all such of the contrary opinion, as have fear of God, and stay upon conscience rather than self-will, I acknowledge myself in christian charity to owe this much of duty, as that I should, to my power, travail to lift this stumbling-block out of their way, that it may not be a let or stay unto them to come unto Christ, at this day by his word calling them. Wherefore, gentle reader, seeing thou dost understand my meaning and the occasion of my doing, I will cease any more to trouble thee, and will turn the residue of my talk unto the author of this writing; with whom I will make my entry there, where he first beginneth to confute the reasons that were alleged, why account should not be made to doctor Cole of that religion that now is taught. In this part I will be the shorter, partly because those things be sufficiently answered in the conference already published, although this writer seemeth to dissemble it; partly, because the questions have more captiousness of words than profit of good matter.

THE DEFENCE

OF

THE TRUTH.

CAP. I.

A.

WHERE you reason against my lord of Salisbury for refusing to bring proof of his doctrine because he was a bishop, and at that time preached before the Queen's grace and her council; you deal somewhat like with him, as you do afterward with the doctors that you do allege. For you first bring your own sense unto their words, and so allege them for your purpose, whereas they mean nothing less. So in the words of the first epistle to doctor Cole, you apply your own sense unto them, and after reason against it, as though it were his meaning. Whether this be to be counted a cavilling, rather than a confuting, I leave to the judgment of other. He never said simply, that he should make no reckoning of his doctrine, because he was a bishop: for he doth the contrary daily, as well in his preaching as otherwise. He never said that the consent of the prince and realm was a sufficient proof of doctrine in christian religion, as you would have men think of him by your reasoning against him. He said this; that, for so much as he was called to the state of a bishop, and at that time uttered before the prince and her council that doctrine, which was confirmed by the authority of the whole realm, he might seem to do unadvisedly, if he should make account thereof to a subject, and especially such a subject as alway hath professed himself to mislike it, and at that time, under pretence of learning, but indeed quarrelling, required a proof thereof. Were it good reason, think you, that a magistrate at the demand of every subject should bring reason to prove any law published by the prince to be good, which the same subject would protest to be an evil and unjust law, and therefore would not obey it? If that should be so, a gap might be opened to every busy person to pick a quarrel against the law. If that should be so, beside other inconveniences, he might seem to submit the judgment of the prince and realm to the misliking of one wayward subject. Which could not be done without great impeachment to the prince's authority, and wisdom of the whole state of the commonweal. That this was his meaning, it may appear in those words, where he saith he might not do it without farther licence. Wherefore in this part of his answer, knowing with whom he had to do, he respected his doctrine, as it was a law confirmed by the prince and states of the realm, and not as it might be a controversy of religion before the law published. *A just cause of his refusal.*

Moreover in that he is orderly called to the state of a bishop (say you what you will to the contrary), he is in possession of the truth; and therefore it were not reason, that he should be requested first to shew his evidence and take upon him the person of the plaintiff: especially toward those men that make exception to his possession, and claim the right thereof themselves. He ought not lightly to give over to you in this point; he ought to acknowledge and stand in defence of that benefit, whereby, through God's word and authority of the prince, he is set in open possession of that which you before usurped. Seeing then it is the plaintiff's part first to shew evidence, and he now (God be thanked) standeth with other as defendant; you do disorderly and contrary to reason to will him to do that, which by order yourself should first do. He proffered openly to give over to you, if you could shew any reasonable evidence for your part out of the scriptures, doctors, or councils: if you refuse it, all men will think that either you have no evidence at all to shew, or else that which you have, is such as you are well assured will not abide the trial.

B.　　In like manner do you mistake his resting upon the negative. You write not against his meaning, but against that yourself conceiveth to be in his words. He said not absolutely, no negative proposition could be proved, neither doth D. Cole find so much fault with him for denying that a negative might be proved, (for himself had so said before,) but with this, that to grieve his adversary he would stay upon the negative, and put you of the contrary part to prove the affirmative. Which was upon good reason done at that time, to the end, as I think, that he might press upon you somewhat nearer[1] than other before had used to

[This word in the original edition is printed *narre*.]

do. For whereas you have untruly borne the world in hand, and make your avaunt continually, that the church hath taught as you do these fifteen hundred years, that the holy scriptures, ancient fathers, and councils do make altogether for your doctrine and against ours; he both wisely and learnedly did see, that there was no way so fit either to drive you from this avaunt, or to declare it evidently to be false, as to rest upon this true negative, that you have no sufficient proof out of the authorities before rehearsed. For thereby he should either force you to shew what you have, which in effect is nothing, or else to confess that the chief points of your doctrine by him recited be, as they are indeed, clean beside the word of God and example of the primitive church: or, if you would not for shame confess it, yet that all men in the end might perceive it is so, when that you neither would nor could bring any sufficient confirmation of the same by the scriptures, old fathers, ancient councils, or allowed example of the church by the space of six hundred years.

The cause why he might justly rest upon the negative.

I will declare the matter by example of those things that yourself taketh in hand to prove. All the preachers of this time teach, that the right use of the Lord's supper is to be celebrated in manner of a communion or feast with company, and that as well the laity as clergy should receive under both kinds. This doctrine they say is according to God's word and use of the primitive church and not the contrary. For proof thereof they allege out of the scripture the evangelists and St Paul, in which appeareth evidently that company was, and both kinds were indifferently used, and no signification at all of the contrary. For the primitive church they bring Justine, Dionysius, Cyprian, Chrysostom and other, declaring in plain words the use of their time to have been so: and affirm that the same ancient fathers never make any evident mention that the contrary manner was used and allowed in the common administration of the sacrament. Contrariwise, you on the other part affirm, that the priest in midst of the congregation may commonly consecrate and receive alone, and that the laity in the communion should receive only the bread and not the cup of the Lord. This doctrine, say you, is according to the scripture and example of the old church; and they that will say the contrary, you count and use as heretics. But when they call upon you to shew some sufficient proof thereof out of the scripture and doctors, you refuse it, cavilling and bidding them prove the contrary. Which is alway the shift of them that have nothing to say.

This is the negative that was stayed upon, that you are not able to prove by the scripture or fathers, that ever the priest used in the church to celebrate alone, as you do in private mass, or that the people in communion was commonly served with the bread only, and not with the cup; and you would have him to prove this negative. As if you should say unto him, Sir, do you prove that we be not able to bring any sufficient testimony out of the fathers. Surely the proof of this negative can be none other but to hold open the books of the bible and doctors to you, and will you to read them over, and see that there is no such proof for your part. If any of your part should say to one of us, as you do in your writing, that no sentence in all the scripture doth justify that we do herein teach, and the party to whom it is spoken would will you to prove it; would you not think he did unlearnedly? would you not think that either he did of purpose seek a shift to cavil, or else indeed had nothing to say? Or if you do think it reasonable, I will learn at your hand how you could prove that negative by all your law or logic? I do scant think you will say, that a man may be orderly required to prove such mere negatives. When a negative, or what kind of negatives, may be proved, I leave to be discussed in some other place, as a question more meet for sophisters in the parvise school at Oxford, than for divines in matters of weight and importance.

After your reasoning against the causes, that, as you say, were alleged not to prove the negative, as it were to lay the ground of your controversy for private masses, ye begin with a distinction, that this term private may be taken after divers sorts; either as contrary to common to many for the commodity thereof, or else as sole receiving by a priest alone without any company. In the first way, you say ye never affirmed mass

CAP. II.

An answer to the distinction of private.

A.

to be private, but to pertain to the behalf of all states and sorts of men, whatsoever they be. Indeed I were to blame and very injurious unto you, if I would deny that ye have been very bountiful in bestowing the benefit of your mass; and especially when money was brought in abundantly. For then ye applied it unto high, to low; to princes, to private persons, to absent, to present; to quick, to dead, to heaven, to hell, yea and to purgatory too: over and beside that ye made it a salve for all sores, and a remedy for all mischiefs. Here were a large field for me to descant upon the divers abuses that you applied it unto, contrary to Christ's institution and ordinance: but that any christian heart may rather yearn and lament to remember so ungodly profanation of the holy sacrament, than to seek occasion pleasantly to dally in the rehearsal and deluding of the infinite vanities thereof. The other signification of private in sole receiving by the priest, not imbarring any that is willing and ready to be partaker with him, ye say the catholic church doth and alway hath taught. And here upon making your proposition, ye require a proof of the affirmative included in the negative; that is, that every priest or any other ought, when he receiveth, to have a company to receive with him.

Why, sir, is this the trust that you would seem to have in the truth of your cause? is this the plain and sound dealing that ye after profess to use? is this the leaving of all shifts, whereby ye may seem to cavil, rather than stay upon the chief proofs of your matter? Who seeth not, that even in the very entrance, mistrusting your quarrel, ye seek a shift as it were by policy to help that which in the open field is not able to defend itself? This was no part of the challenge (as you term it). This is not that ye pretend so earnestly to prove. The matter is of private masses, and you make your issue in sole receiving. Is there no difference, think you, between sole receiving and private mass? Doth every one that receiveth alone say a private mass? Then may not only priests say mass, but also, by your own authorities after brought in, laymen and women also. And yet your reasoning in the residue of your treatise is such, as if it were a sufficient proof of private mass, to shew that some men and women in certain cases received alone in the primitive church. But of your arguments afterward. In this place ye shall give me leave to find that fault in you that Tully in the beginning of his Offices layeth to Panetius; who, intending to write of duty in behaviour, omitteth the definition of the same: whereas every reasonable discourse ought to proceed of a brief declaration of that which is in controversy. If ye had this done, I doubt not but ye would rather have plucked your pen from the paper, than have meddled with the matter that ye are now entered into.

I will therefore shew you out of your own authors, what I take your private mass to be. It is a sacrifice of the body

What private mass is.

B.

and blood of Christ, used in the church in place of the Lord's supper, by one priest alone offered to God the Father for the sins of quick and dead: which, without any to participate with him, he may apply to the benefit of what persons and things he listeth. That it is a sacrifice of Christ's body, that it is used in place of the Lord's supper, that one may offer it for quick and dead, that it is in the priest's power to apply it, all your sort do not only without resistance easily confess, but without reason stoutly defend. Therefore I shall not need to make any further proof of the parts of this description. I do therefore take private mass to be, not only as you and some other patrons of your cause of late years have wrested it, since the ministers of God's truth in this latter time have driven you to the best shifts of interpretation; but as it was commonly used in the world before, and as it is set forth in your schoolmen, to the great defacing of Christ's death and passion. And yet ye shall not think that we of truth can or ought to yield to the best of your interpretations that ever I could hear.

Of this private mass that I have now declared to you, the challenge, that ye take so grievously, was made; and therein do I also at this time join issue with you, and say, that neither you nor any of your part will ever be able to prove the same by the holy scriptures, ancient fathers, or allowed councils; yea, and because you urge the negative, that, with God's help, we will abundantly prove the contrary. This will I do quietly and calmly, without storming or tempestuous blustering either at you or at your doctrine; as one most glad to bring you again to that heavenly truth of the gospel, which, under the blasphemous names of falsehood and fantasy, you declare yourself to have forsaken.

In the residue of your discourse ye would seem to take from us the true and right rule to reform the church of Christ, that is, to prove that in doctrines and use of the sacraments all things should not be reduced to the pattern of the apostles' time and the primitive church. Herein you do as they are wont, whose conscience doth prick them to have done amiss. For such alway draw back and lurk out of the light; being loath to come there where they know that truth would be tried. Even so you, fearing to be found faulty, would wring us from that rule whereby all truth in doctrine ought to be examined. To this purpose ye may seem to bring three reasons. One is a rolling in of a rabble of such examples as no reasonable man would deny unto you. The second is a resembling of the primitive church unto an infant in the swaddling clouts; and this latter time to a tall man of perfect years and ripe age. The third is the comparison of the times and the fervent charity that then was with the key-cold charity that now is.

As touching the first, I cannot choose but greatly marvel at your manner of reasoning; which endeavour to prove the contrary of

CAP. III.

A.

that that no man did ever affirm. Did ye ever hear of any that would have all things without exception reduced to that very form of the world that was in the primitive church? And yet your examples tendeth to the proof of nothing else. But you pleased yourself so trimly in the device of those pretty taunts and odious suspicions, as you would rather prove that no man denied, than leave them out of your writing. Your mind was by like to make the world think that we purposed, under colour of reformation, to bring all things in common, to suppress christian princes, to pull temporalties from bishops; to make men forbear stifled meats, to bring infants again to communion, &c. If ye thought it to be true, ye were wickedly persuaded; if ye did not think it, ye did maliciously to write it. As for kings and princes, we must leave [them] to the government of God's providence, and commonweals to be ruled by their good and wholesome laws. For the teaching of the gospel taketh not away civil order and policy. But religion, which is the worshipping of God, must be examined chiefly by the word of God, appointed to be the very touchstone thereof, partly also by the state of that time, which, in all reason, may seem to be farthest from corruption.

Herein are to be considered two kinds of things; truth of doctrines, and right use of the sacraments, as things in the church most necessary; rites and ceremonies for order's sake, as things mean and indifferent. In doctrine there is but one verity, and but one right use of the sacraments. Therefore they should be always one at all times, and then are most likely to be least corrupted when they are nighest the time they were first ordained in. As for ceremonies, they may by discretion be altered, as person, place, state of time and other circumstances shall give occasion. For the use of ceremonies therefore and things indifferent, we do not bind you to the apostles' time and the primitive church. *What things ought to be reformed to the state of the primitive church, and why.*

But if the use of the sacraments be either by ignorance corrupted, either with false opinions depraved, or with superstitious ceremonies defaced, is it not full time, think you, to call for redress according to the scripture and primitive church? So to do we have good example in Christ himself, and in his apostle St Paul. When Christ would purge the law from pharisaical mitigations and interpretations, he had recourse to the first fountain and original: saying, *Dictum est veteribus, &c. Ego autem dico vobis.* So he reduced all to the first fountain. In the matter of divorcement he alleged not the rabbins and late writers of Jews, but said, *Ab initio non fuit sic:* counting whatsoever was added to the first ordinance of the law to be a corruption of it. St Paul minding to redress the abuse of this sacrament of the Lord's supper, even in this point, that they took it in parts and not together, bringeth the institution of Christ from the beginning, and saith: "This have I received of the Lord:" willing to alter nothing therein. Matt. v.

[1Cor. xi. 23.]

The like doth St Cyprian, *Epist. ad Cæcilium*, against *Aquarios*. "We must not hearken," saith he, "what other did before us, but what Christ first did, that was before all[1]." And here he speaketh of the same sacrament, and against them that abused it contrary to the first foundation, were they never so holy. This, Tertullian, also, taketh to be a sure rule against all heresies and abuses, who saith in this wise: "This reason is of force against all heresies. That is true that was first ordained, and that is corrupted that is after done[2]." And Cyprian in the same epistle before mentioned, "Hereof," saith he, "arise divisions in the church, because we seek not to the head, nor have recourse to the fountain, nor keep the commandments of the heavenly master[3]." Therefore, seeing it is so good a rule in religion to resort to the first institution, we also without any just reproach may require to have the sacraments reformed

[1 Quare si solus Christus audiendus est, non debemus attendere, quid alius ante nos faciendum putaverit, sed quid, qui ante omnes est, Christus prior fecerit.—Cypr. Ep. ad Cæcil. Op. ed. Fell. Ox. 1682. Pt. ii. p. 155.]

[2 Quo peræque adversus universas hæreses jam hinc præjudicatum sit, id esse verum quodcunque primum ; id esse adulterum quodcunque posterius.— Tertull. Adv. Praxeam, c. 2. Op. ed. Semler. Halæ Magd. 1770. Vol. ii. p. 147.]

[3 The passage of Cyprian here referred to is not in his Letter to Cæcilius, but in his tract, *Of the Unity of the Church ;* and is as follows:— Hoc [*i. e.* the prevalence of heresies and schisms among Christians] eo fit, dum ad veritatis originem non reditur, nec caput quæritur, nec magistri cœlestis doctrina servatur.—Cypr. De Unitate Eccles. Op. ed. cit. Pt. i. p. 105.]

according to the scripture and the primitive church.

But you think, perhaps, although for shame ye may not say it, that their successors in elder age of the church were of more wisdom and discretion, and knew better what they had to do than the apostles and old fathers. Thereto tendeth your similitude of bringing a tall man again to his swaddling clouts; therein resembling the primitive church to infancy, and this latter time to ripe age and discretion. This is not your only similitude. It is much in the mouths of such as maintain your doctrine. But, I assure you, it was never invented without the spirit of antichrist; nor cannot be maintained without blasphemy against Christ, and singular reproach of his apostles and their successors. If that time were the state of infancy in the church, when Christ himself instructed, when his apostles taught, when the holy fathers governed next their time; then we must needs reckon Christ, the apostles, the fathers, to be infants in religion, to be babes in government of the church, not to be able so well to see what was convenient in the use of the sacrament as their posterity were. Can any christian man's heart fall into that cogitation without fear of God's wrath and displeasure? And yet that must needs follow upon this defence of your doctrine. I pray you, when hath a man best discretion to rule himself? Will ye not say when he is most endued with the use of reason and wisdom? When had the church of God such abundant wisdom and knowledge of

B.

That the primitive church was not of the state of infancy.

his heavenly mysteries? When was it endued with so plentiful graces of the Holy Ghost, as it was in [the] time of the apostles and first fathers? Did it not appear in their pure life, in their fervent zeal, in their miraculous working? And will you then, to defend your ceremonies, affirm that time to be the state of infancy in the church? Do you not remember, that immediately after ye attribute to the primitive church passing fervent charity, with exceeding holiness of life and contempt of the world: to this latter time key-cold charity, slack devotion, love of the world, and contempt of virtue? Whereof I pray you cometh this? Not because in the first time they were strong in godliness, abundant in lively spirit and grace of God; and we now feeble and faint to all virtuous doing, lacking wisdom, and as it were doting for age? For what other cause was young age of children called infancy, than for that it had not the use of the tongue, nor could not speak? But the primitive church could speak, and continually declare the good will of God and his great benefits to his people. St Paul spake with a loud voice and a strong spirit: "Woe be to me, if I preach not the gospel." The same was the voice of all the old fathers and godly men in the beginning. They were occupied in nothing but either in teaching and confirming truth, or in reproving and defacing falsehood and heresy; but after six hundred years the prelates of the church well near clean lost their voices. Wealth of the world, honour and

[1Cor. xi. 16.]

riches had stopped their mouths in such sort, that within few years it came to pass, that it was a rare matter, and almost a reproach, to see a bishop in the pulpit, and hear him speak to the people. Wherefore ye cannot so aptly resemble the primitive church to infancy, as ye may this latter time to doting old age; wherein they that should do nothing but preach the word of God and teach the people, have either clean lost the use of their speech through infancy and ignorance, or else babble they wot not what, through dotage and folly. That ye may not think me to speak of stomach more than truth, read the histories of this latter time, read those that write particularly of the bishops of Rome, see how many be praised for preaching to the people and for teaching the word of God, either by speaking or writing: so that they may not only seem for age to have lost the strength of their voice, but, as it were with a palsy, to have lost the use of their hands, unless it were in writing of decrees or fingering of pence.

In that ye attribute unto the primitive church so good devotion, so earnest zeal, so fervent charity, and thereby that they came daily to the receiving of the sacrament; it is most true that ye say. But you must again consider, that the often frequenting of the Lord's supper, by grace therein conferred, did both breed and increase that same lively faith and fervent charity, that in mutual love and contempt of the world so flourishingly did shew itself in them. So that their earnest zeal did not so much cause them to come

C.
An answer to the comparison of this time with the primitive church.

often to the Lord's supper, as the often frequenting thereof did increase their so great zeal and charity. For by that means it was always fresh in their memory, not only by hearing, but also by feeling in themselves, that they were all members of one body, all the children of one Father, all delivered out of bondage by one ransom, all fed with one food, and nourished at one table. And therefore that it was as meet and necessary for them to embrace one another, as for one limb of the body to help another; for one brother to love another; one delivered out of thraldom to rejoice with the other; one household companion to tender the good estate of the other.

Therefore that key-cold charity, that you say, and truly say, doth reign in these days, may not more justly be attributed to any one thing than to your private mass. For thereby the common use and frequentation of the holy sacrament of unity, love, and concord, hath been taken from among the people of God; being persuaded by you that it was sufficient for them to be present in the church when one of you alone did say a private mass. You lay the cause of private mass upon the key-cold charity of the people; (and perhaps the first occasion came thereof indeed;) but your scalding hot and fireburning charity may be more justly charged with the continuance thereof. And therefore the people of God may worthily cry out upon the chief masters and maintainers of it; for all the mischief and devilishness, either in naughtiness of life, or corruption of doctrine,

[margin: Cold charity is not so much cause of private mass, as private mass is of cold charity.]

that the church hath been drowned in this certain hundred years, may seem to be drawn in first by that occasion. "Hasten you," saith Ignatius, "to the sacrament of thanksgiving and to the glory of God. For when that is continually frequented, all the powers of the devil are expelled[1]." Then must it of necessity be, that the slack use of the same doth bring in weakness of faith, coldness of charity, contempt of virtue, love of the world, and the whole heap of those things that the devil most desireth and chiefly sheweth his power in. Therefore not without a cause that perpetual enemy of mankind quickly did seek occasion, even in St Paul's time, to corrupt the right use of this sacrament, and bring them to factions in receiving of it. He did well see of how great force it was to maintain concord, love, and charity; which is, as it were, the very cognizance of a christian man. For that cause he endeavouring, as he doth alway, traitorously to train away the servants of God, first alway by the abuse of this sacrament of unity, he, as it were, cutteth off the cognizance from their liveries; that, not being known whose soldiers they are, he may the sooner convey them into his camp, and there put on his badge of hatred, malice, and dissension. Your fault therefore in furthering his endea-

[1 Σπουδάζετε οὖν πυκνότερον συνέρχεσθαι εἰς εὐχαριστίαν Θεοῦ καὶ εἰς δόξαν· ὅτ' ἂν γὰρ πυκνῶς ἐπὶ τὸ αὐτὸ γίνεσθε, καθαιροῦνται αἱ δυνάμεις τοῦ Σατανᾶ, καὶ λύεται ὁ ὄλεθρος αὐτοῦ ἐν τῇ ὁμονοίᾳ ὑμῶν τῆς πίστεως.—IGNAT. Ep. ad Ephes. §. 13. Apud Patr. Apost. ed. Jacobson. Oxon. 1838. Vol. II. p. 284.]

vour cannot be excused; but is to be taken of christian people as very grievous and heinous.

An objection. But ye will say, that the priest doth not imbar any that will communicate; that he would rejoice to see them dispose themselves unto it; that they do lament to see *The answer.* the contrary. These be fair words without any sound truth at all. I assure you, sir, if the matter were so indeed unfeignedly, and not you, by force of truth against you, driven to seek that interpretation for a shift, your sole receiving had been much more tolerable. But when, I pray you, did any of you use in private masses to call for the people? to reprove their slackness? to shew them the danger of being present and not receiving? to tell them of the great commodities that cometh by the use of it? When did any of you stand at the altar as Chrysostom did[1], and cry for the people to be partakers; declaring to them, that, in being present at this heavenly feast as gazers and no receivers, they did run into the indignation and displeasure of God; even as they which, being bid of a prince to a feast, and coming into the house where tables be laid and furnished with meat, will stand looking on and eat none of it, must of necessity greatly displease that prince, whose provision and furniture they do so disgrace. When, I say, did any of you follow his example, whom unjustly ye bring for defence of your error? Is not the whole man-

[1 See Chrysostom. Comm. in Ep. ad Eph. Hom. 3. §. 5. Op. ed. Bened. Tom. XI. pp. 23, 4.]

ner of your mass contrary to this? Do you not turn from the people? Do you not whisper softly to yourself? Do you not use a strange language, that neither the people, neither the priests sometime, do understand? Do you not persuade them, that they may have the benefit of it, though they receive not the sacrament? Chrysostom proveth, and other doctors witnesseth, that those that be present and not receive, do wickedly and impudently; and you teach that, being present and not receiving, they do holily and godly. If this be not to teach contrary to the fathers and to the primitive church, I cannot tell what may be contrary. To conclude, therefore, if the people be slack and not well disposed to frequenting of the sacrament, the fault is in you. And you, whose duty it was to warn and instruct them, shall make account for their decay and perishing in their negligence.

But the effect of your argument, wherein ye allege the cold charity of the people, thereby to drive us necessarily to grant sole receiving, tendeth to this end: if their devotion be so little, as they will not with calling and exhortation dispose themselves to receive, whether then we will (as your phrase is) pull the priest from the altar. First acknowledge and amend that fault of your mass, wherein appeareth neither calling and exhortation, nor gesture and language fit for that purpose. Then I say it were better not only to pluck him from the altar, but also to cast him out of the church too, rather than he should under that pretence both himself continually

D.

alter the institution of Christ, and also cause the people being present, by Chrysostom's witness, to run into God's displeasure. Moreover, this key-cold charity, that ye say the people's hearts be frozen with, doth it stretch unto priests or no? Is their devotion any hotter? surely their burning zeal, that of late time they have used, proveth, and their whole behaviour to the world witnesseth, that right devotion and true charity is even as little among your massing priests as among the ignorant people. How happeneth, then, that they do so often frequent the sacrament in these days? There were never half so many masses (though ye take mass for the communion) as there is in this time. Ye shall never read in the primitive church that they had more than one celebration in a day, unless the church were so little, that it would not receive the communicants (as Leo in a certain epistle mentioneth[1]). But in your churches ye have sometime twenty or thirty, and yet

[1 Ut autem in omnibus observantia nostra concordet, illud quoque volumus custodiri, ut cum solemnior festivitas conventum populi numerosioris indixerit, et ad eam tanta fidelium multitudo convenerit, quam recipere basilica simul una non possit, sacrificii oblatio indubitanter iteretur: ne his tantum admissis ad hanc devotionem, qui primi advenerint, videantur hi, qui postmodum confluxerint, non recepti, cum plenum pietatis atque rationis sit, ut quoties basilicam, in qua agitur, præsentia novæ plebis impleverit, toties sacrificium subsequens offeratur. Necesse est autem, ut quædam pars populi sua devotione privetur, si, *unius tantum missæ more servato*, sacrificium offerre non possit [possint], nisi qui prima diei parte convenerint.—LEON. MAGN. Ep. ad Dioscor. Ep. Alex. Ep. 81. inter Op. Leon. Magn. &c. ed. Theoph. Raynaud. Lugd. 1633. fol. pp. 149, 150.]

not two communicants at any of them. Ye must then confess either a great and horrible abuse of the sacrament, or else that your priests' devotion now is much more than in the primitive church.

But ye object, that priests are bounden of duty to the daily frequentation of it, and the people left free. That would I fain learn at your hand, and see some good proof of the scripture for the same. But I answer that you, which say we have no colour of scripture for that we herein defend, have less than a light shadow to hide your false assertion in; and that in this ye speak clean beside the word of God. Christ's institution was general, and his commandment therein stretcheth as well to the people as to the priests. "Take, eat, drink you all of this; do this in remembrance of me," bindeth the people as well as the priests. That ye may not reply, that all which were present were priests, because they were apostles, and so apply the sacrament unto priests of necessity, and to the people upon free pleasure, understand you that St Paul, a good interpreter of Christ's mind, applieth the same to the whole congregation of Corinth; where it is certain were both ministers and common people.

As for the duty of ministration, whereby perhaps ye think priests more bounden, ye should not attribute more to the priest ministering than to Christ ministering. But Christ took the bread, gave thanks, brake it, gave it to them present, willed them therein to remember his death. Then the priest in his ministration must do as Christ

E.

[Matt. xxvi. 26, 27. Luke xxii. 19.]

[1 Cor. xi. 23, et seq.]

did, and no otherwise; that is, to take, give thanks, break, and give unto the people. But why should he break it, or how should he distribute it, if there be none present to receive it? So that hereon I conclude the priest is not bound to minister, if there be none to receive. If we had no scripture at all to prove that the priest should not receive without company, if ye did give us the overthrow in that, yet could ye not triumph therein, as though ye had won the field. It were but the shifting back of one wing of the battle, which ye might overthrow, and yet miss of your purpose. Our contention is for private mass, and your purpose is to prove your use of private mass to be good; of which sole receiving is but one part, and yet have [you] not sufficiently concluded that neither. For it followeth not to say, the priest in case of necessity, when none will receive, may take the sacrament alone; therefore he may do it without necessity, when he may have other to communicate with him. Do you never receive alone in your mass, but ye be driven for lack of other? How happeneth then that in one church ye shall have at one time seven or eight massing in sundry corners, where they might communicate all together; as the manner was of the ministers in the primitive church? Is it of necessity, or a purposed altering of Christ's institution, when that ye turn it from a communion and supper, to a work that one man may do to the benefit of many; and thereby have made it a merchandise to buy and sell for your own gain?

What colour or shadow have you for this in the scripture? Surely, were my moderation much more than yours is, I could not choose but term this, not an itching folly, but an impudent wilfulness, so plainly to go against the express and appointed form of the sacrament.

Because ye urge so earnestly to have due proof against sole receiving by the priest, if the people will not communicate, I will shew you some reasons. But before I enter into that, I must warn you once again, that, if our reasons were not so well able to prove necessity, yet could you not conclude your purpose, for that your private mass is nothing less than necessity. In necessity many things may be granted, that otherwise are not tolerable. The thief, that Christ at his death witnessed should be with him in paradise, was never baptized; being excluded by necessity. The ancient histories make mention of divers martyrs, that died before they were baptized, being excluded by necessity. And yet is this sentence never the less true: Baptism is necessary to a christian man. Likewise if we should grant your case of necessity, yet is this sentence alway true: The supper of the Lord, in the ordinary use of it, ought of necessity to have communicants to be partakers of it.

But ye shall hear the foundation of our proofs against sole receiving by the priest in place of ministry: and they shall not be gaily garnished with colours and amplifications, to make them appear more goodly than they be, but plainly and nakedly set forth, that

F.

even the meanest may see what force and strength they have. For I write not this so much to you, whom I know not, as to a number partly of unlearned persons, partly young men learned, but not much conversant in the scriptures, to whose hands these your writings being brought hath borne a greater face of proof than any man meanly conversant in the controversies of this time can acknowledge to be in them. Our proof is this. In the celebration of this sacrament of the Lord's supper we ought to do that only, and nothing else, that Christ the author of it did in his institution. But in Christ's institution appeareth neither sole receiving, nor ministering under one kind. Therefore in celebration of this sacrament neither sole receiving nor ministering under one kind ought to be used.

Proofs against private mass, out of the scripture.

The major is [by] St Cyprian proved at large and much stayed upon in his epistle, *Ad Cæcilium de Sacramento Sanguinis*, in the beginning whereof he seemeth to signify, that by inspiration he was admonished of God, to advertise men only to do as Christ did in the institution of his sacrament. "I thought it," saith he, "both godly and necessary to write, if any man continue in this error," he meaneth using water only in the sacrament instead of wine, "that he, seeing the light, do return to the root and beginning of the Lord's ordinance and institution. And think not that I do this upon my own fantasy, or any human judgment, &c.; but when one is charged by the inspiration and commandment of God, it is necessary for a faith-

ful servant to obey: being holden excused
with all men, because he taketh nothing upon
him arrogantly, that is compelled to fear the
displeasure of God, if he do not as he is bid.
Do you know, therefore, that we be admonished, that in offering the sacrament of the
Lord's blood, his own institution should be
kept, and no other thing be done than that
the Lord did first for us himself[1]?" No
man can make any exception to this proposition, unless he will clean weaken Cyprian's
reason against those abusers of the sacrament. And then shall we have no ground to
stay upon, but every gloss or interpretation
upon human pretences shall be admitted.

This assertion of Cyprian is confirmed by
Ambrose upon the first to the Corinthians.
There he saith, that they receive the sacra-
ment unworthily which celebrate otherwise

[1] Quoniam quidam vel ignoranter vel simpliciter
in calice Dominico sanctificando, et plebi minis-
trando, non hoc faciunt quod Jesus Christus, Dominus et Deus noster, sacrificii hujus auctor et doctor,
fecit et docuit, religiosum pariter ac necessarium duxi
has ad vos literas facere, ut si quis in isto errore adhuc teneatur, veritatis luce perspecta, ad radicem atque originem traditionis Dominicæ revertatur. Nec
nos putes, frater carissime, nostra et humana conscri-
bere, aut ultronea voluntate hoc nobis audacter assu-
mere, cum mediocritatem nostram semper humili et
verecunda moderatione teneamus; sed quando aliquid
Deo aspirante et mandante præcipitur, necesse est
Domino servus fidelis obtemperet; excusatus apud
omnes, quod nihil sibi arroganter assumat, qui offen-
sam Domini timere compellitur, nisi faciat quod ju-
betur. Admonitos autem nos scias, ut in calice offe-
rendo Dominica traditio servetur, neque aliud fiat a
nobis, quam quod pro nobis Dominus prior fecerit.—
CYPR. Ep. ad Cæcilium. *init.* Ep. 63. ed. Fell. Ox.
1682. Pt. II. p. 148.]

than the Lord delivered it. "For he," saith Ambrose, "cannot be devout, which presumeth to do it otherwise than the author hath taught[1]." Yea, and addeth that we shall make an account how we have used it.

For the proof of the minor, let us consider the history thereof as it is set out in the evangelists. In the celebration of the sacrament used by Christ there appeareth two parts; the matter and the form: the matter is bread and the body of Christ, wine and the blood of Christ; of which he that altereth or taketh away any, doth alter and maim Christ's institution, as appeareth by Cyprian. The form of ministering the sacrament must be taken out of Christ's doings. At that time it was taken, blessed with thanksgiving, broken, distributed, eaten, drunken, charge given to remember Christ and his death. Therefore he that altereth or taketh away any of these things, maimeth the form of Christ's institution, and breaketh Cyprian's rule. Moreover the force of these words, "Gave to them present," doth bind to a company; because it signifieth a bestowing of the death of Christ not to one, but to many. Therefore in Luke he giveth an express commandment of distributing, as he

[1 Indignum dicit esse Domino, qui aliter mysterium celebrat, quam ab eo traditum est. Non enim potest devotus esse, qui aliter præsumit, quam datum est ab auctore. Ideoque præmonet ut secundum ordinem traditum devota mens sit accedentis ad eucharistiam Domini; quoniam futurum est judicium, ut quemadmodum accedit unusquisque, reddat causas in die Domini Jesu Christi.—PSEUDO-AMBROSII Comment. in 1 Cor. xi. 27. Inter Ambros. Op. ed. Bened. Vol. II. Append. col. 149.]

doth of eating and drinking, saying, "Take you this, and divide it among you." But how can he divide it, if there be not a company to receive it; unless we should, to the deluding of Christ's ordinance, make such a fantastical breaking and dividing, as you do in your mass? For therein, by Sergius'[1] decree, ye break it into three parts: the one of which ye let fall into the wine, which there soaked signifieth the body of Christ raised from death, and sitting in the glory; the other dry part, that the priest eateth, signifieth the body of Christ being upon the earth; the third part, which is wont to tarry on the altar to the end of mass, signifieth the dead in the sepulchres until the day of judgment. O great vanities wherewith God punisheth the rashness of foolish men following their own fantasies, and leaving his holy word!

[Luke xxii. 17.]

But to return to the proof of the matter. I will follow Cyprian's example, and confirm the manner of Christ's institution by the testimony of St Paul. In him I find two arguments. One is in these words, *Unus panis unum corpus multi sumus: nam omnes de eodem pane participamus*. Which words the holy fathers interpret-

[1 Cor. x. 17.]

[1 Triforme est corpus Domini. Pars oblatæ, in calicem missa, corpus Christi, quod jam resurrexit, monstrat. Pars comesta, ambulans adhuc super terram. Pars in altari usque ad missæ finem remanens, corpus jacens in sepulchro: quia usque ad finem seculi corpora sanctorum in sepulchris erunt.—SERGIUS PAPA in Gratiani Decret. Pt. III. De consecr. dist. 2. c. 22. Corp. Jur. Canon. ed. Col. Munat. 1783. Tom. I. col. 1170.]

ing, call the Lord's holy supper a sacrament of unity; because that as the bread consisteth of many grains, and the wine [is] made of many grapes, so we, that be partakers of that one loaf and one cup, should be knit together in love and charity, as the members and parts of one mystical body. Wherefore Chrysostom noteth, that it is not said, this eateth of one bread, and he of another; but all be partakers of one bread: and addeth why we be one loaf and one body:—" Because of the common participation that we have of the sacrament[1]." This signification is clean taken away by private mass; the use whereof may seem rather to be a sacrament of separation and dispension[2], as after shall more appear. The second argument out of St Paul is, where to the Corinthians he reprehendeth the abuse of the Lord's supper brought in by dissension and factions that were among them. Whereby it came to pass, that one company would not tarry for another to communicate, but one sort would receive without another. Against this abuse he allegeth the institution of Christ, signifying the same to be against such receiving in parts, and therefore exhorteth them to tarry until the congregation

[1 Cor. xi. 20—34.]

[1 Αὐτό ἐσμεν ἐκεῖνο τὸ σῶμα· τί γάρ ἐστιν ὁ ἄρτος; σῶμα Χριστοῦ. τί δὲ γίνονται οἱ μεταλαμβάνοντες; σῶμα Χριστοῦ. οὐχὶ σώματα πολλὰ, ἀλλὰ σῶμα ἕν......οὐ γὰρ ἐξ ἑτέρου μὲν σώματος σὺ, ἐξ ἑτέρου δὲ ἐκεῖνος τρέφεται, ἀλλ' ἐκ τοῦ αὐτοῦ πάντες. διὸ καὶ ἐπήγαγεν· οἱ γὰρ πάντες ἐκ τοῦ ἑνὸς ἄρτου μετέχομεν.—CHRYSOST. in Ep. 1. ad Corinth. Hom. xxiv. §. 2. Op. ed. Bened. Tom. x. pp. 213, 214.]

[2 ? dispersion.]

came together, that they might receive according to Christ's institution. That this was St Paul's mind, it appeareth by his first proposition and reason, and by the conclusion that he addeth in the end. "When ye come together," saith he, "ye cannot eat the Lord's supper;" where first it is to be noted, that to the celebration of the sacrament they resorted together, and were not privately in sundry corners. He addeth the reason why they could not at their meetings celebrate the Lord's supper. "Because every man is occupied in eating his own supper." Herein Paul blameth them, not only for immoderate feeding of their own meat, but also for the disordered using of the Lord's supper in parts; whereas they should be together, as Christ and his apostles were. This he declareth more plainly in that conclusion, that he inferreth upon the rehearsal of Christ's words in ordering the sacrament. For he saith: "Therefore, my brethren, when ye come together to eat the Lord's supper, do you tarry one for another." What can more plainly declare that St Paul took the right use of the sacrament to be a common receiving together, and not a several use by one man alone? As if he had said: In Christ's supper ye see the master together with the disciples, the table and the meat common to all; not so much as Judas the traitor excluded; one loaf and one cup distributed among the whole company. Therefore when ye come together, ye must imitate the concord and equality that he then used. If he thought it an abuse in the Corinthians to receive in parts, he would count it a far greater abuse for ten or twelve to receive each of them severally in one church, at one time, as though they were of divers religions, or members of divers mystical bodies. If the Corinthians in receiving by parts were blamed of Paul, for that they seemed one to contemn another, may not priests be as justly blamed because they seem in their private mass to disdain and contemn the people? I will now therefore conclude with Cyprian's words: "If so be both it be ordained by Christ, and the same confirmed by the apostle, that we should do in this sacrament as our Lord did, we find that we keep not that is commanded, if we do otherwise than Christ did[1]." Seeing then Christ used company in ordaining the sacrament of that holy feast and supper, priests also ought to have company in ministering the same.

Proofs against private mass, out of the fathers.

For the authority of the primitive church to confirm that this is the right use of the sacrament, I will in this place bring in only two witnesses; which shall not speak of this matter lightly or by the way, but of very purpose declare the manner that then was used among the people of God, allowed and confirmed by godly and holy fathers. Insomuch that if any other manner had been then used, they could not have

[[1] Quod si et a Domino præcipitur, et ab Apostolo ejus hoc idem confirmatur et traditur, ut quotiescunque biberimus in commemorationem Domini, hoc faciamus, quod fecit et Dominus; invenimus, non observari a nobis quod mandatum est, nisi eadem quæ Dominus fecit, nos quoque faciamus.—CYPR. Epist. ad Cæcil. Op. ed. cit. p. 152.]

omitted the same; especially seeing they professed to declare the manner of Christians therein. Justin the martyr, in his Apology, describeth it thus[1]: "After prayer we salute each other with a kiss: then bread and the cup mixed with water is brought to the chief brother, which after he hath taken, giving praise and thanks unto the Father of all, in the name of the Son and Holy Ghost, for a space he continueth in thanks-

[1 Ἀλλήλους φιλήματι ἀσπαζόμεθα παυσάμενοι τῶν εὐχῶν. Ἔπειτα προσφέρεται τῷ προεστῶτι τῶν ἀδελφῶν ἄρτος καὶ ποτήριον ὕδατος καὶ κράματος, καὶ οὗτος λαβὼν αἶνον καὶ δόξαν τῷ Πατρὶ τῶν ὅλων διὰ τοῦ ὀνόματος τοῦ Υἱοῦ καὶ τοῦ Πνεύματος τοῦ ἁγίου ἀναπέμπει, καὶ εὐχαριστίαν ὑπὲρ τοῦ κατηξιῶσθαι τούτων παρ' αὐτοῦ ἐπὶ πολὺ ποιεῖται· οὗ συντελέσαντος τὰς εὐχὰς καὶ τὴν εὐχαριστίαν πᾶς ὁ παρὼν λαὸς ἐπευφημεῖ λέγων, Ἀμήν. Τὸ δὲ ἀμὴν τῇ ἑβραΐδι φωνῇ τὸ γένοιτο σημαίνει. Εὐχαριστήσαντος δὲ τοῦ προεστῶτος καὶ ἐπευφημήσαντος παντὸς τοῦ λαοῦ, οἱ καλούμενοι παρ' ἡμῖν διάκονοι διδόασιν ἑκάστῳ τῶν παρόντων μεταλαβεῖν ἀπὸ τοῦ εὐχαριστηθέντος ἄρτου καὶ οἴνου καὶ ὕδατος, καὶ τοῖς οὐ παροῦσιν ἀποφέρουσι. Καὶ ἡ τροφὴ αὕτη καλεῖται παρ' ἡμῖν εὐχαριστία......Καὶ τῇ τοῦ ἡλίου λεγομένῃ ἡμέρᾳ πάντων κατὰ πόλεις ἢ ἀγροὺς μενόντων ἐπὶ τὸ αὐτὸ συνέλευσις γίνεται, καὶ τὰ ἀπομνημονεύματα τῶν ἀποστόλων ἢ τὰ συγγράμματα τῶν προφητῶν ἀναγινώσκεται, μέχρις ἐγχωρεῖ. Εἶτα παυσαμένου τοῦ ἀναγινώσκοντος, ὁ προεστὼς διὰ λόγου τὴν νουθεσίαν καὶ πρόκλησιν τῆς τῶν καλῶν τούτων μιμήσεως ποιεῖται. Ἔπειτα ἀνιστάμεθα κοινῇ πάντες καὶ εὐχὰς πέμπομεν. Καὶ, ὡς προέφημεν, παυσαμένων ἡμῶν τῆς εὐχῆς ἄρτος προσφέρεται καὶ οἶνος καὶ ὕδωρ, καὶ ὁ προεστὼς εὐχὰς ὁμοίως καὶ εὐχαριστίας, ὅση δύναμις αὐτῷ, ἀναπέμπει, καὶ ὁ λαὸς ἐπευφημεῖ λέγων τὸ ἀμήν· καὶ ἡ διάδοσις καὶ ἡ μετάληψις ἀπὸ τῶν εὐχαριστηθέντων ἑκάστῳ γίνεται, καὶ τοῖς οὐ παροῦσι διὰ τῶν διακόνων πέμπεται.—JUST. MART. Apol. 1. §§ 65—67. Op. ed. Otto. Jen. 1847. 8vo. Tom. I. Pt. I. pp. 154—60.]

giving. After prayers and thanksgiving, the whole company saith Amen. When the minister's giving of thanks, and the people's well-wishing is finished, those which we call deacons give part of the bread and cup, over which thanks is given, unto every one that is present, yea, and suffer the same to be carried to them that be absent. This nourishment we call Eucharistiam, the sacrament of thanksgiving." A little after he declareth the same thing again. "On Sunday," saith he, "companies of the town and country come together, where lessons of the prophets and apostles be read. When the clerk ceaseth, the minister exhorteth and allureth them to the imitation of so holy things. After, we all arise and pray. Then (as I said) bread and wine mixed with water is brought forth, and the chief minister, so much as he can, prayeth, and giveth thanks, the people singing Amen. Then the things consecrated are distributed to all present, and be sent by the deacons to those that be absent." The same form and manner of celebration of the sacrament, with very little difference, is witnessed by Dionysius; who in *Ecclesiastica Hierarchia*, after he hath described a few other circumstances, and noted that only they tarried in the church which were meet for the sight and communion of the divine and holy sacrament, addeth this: "After he hath shewn the gifts of those divine works, he both cometh to the communion of the same himself, and also allureth other. When the divine communion is both taken and given, it endeth in holy thanksgiving[1]."

Would a man desire any plainer testimony of the use of the Lord's supper in the primitive church? Doth not all things agree with the institution of Christ, and example of the apostle? Is here any conjecture either of the laity receiving under one kind? or of sole receiving by the priest? or of sacrificing the body and blood of Christ for quick and dead? Is here any word or ceremony that signifieth such use to have been at that time? Yet (as I said) these men write not of this matter by the way, but of purpose undertook to shew the manner of the church

[1 Ἑξῆς δὲ, διὰ τῶν λειτουργῶν ἡ τῶν ἁγιογράφων δέλτων ἀνάγνωσις ἀκολούθως γίνεται· καὶ μετὰ ταύτας ἔξω γίγνονται τῆς ἱερᾶς περιοχῆς οἱ κατηχούμενοι, καὶ πρὸς αὐτοῖς οἱ ἐνεργούμενοι, καὶ οἱ ἐν μετανοίᾳ ὄντες μένουσι δὲ οἱ τῆς τῶν θείων ἐποψίας καὶ κοινωνίας ἄξιοι......καὶ τὰς δωρεὰς τῶν θεουργιῶν ὑποδείξας, εἰς κοινωνίαν αὐτῶν ἱερὰν αὐτός τε ἔρχεται, καὶ τοὺς ἄλλους προτρέπεται. Μετασχὼν δὲ καὶ μεταδοὺς τῆς θεαρχικῆς κοινωνίας, εἰς εὐχαριστίαν ἱερὰν καταλήγει. And a little further on he adds:—Ταῦτα τοῖς ἱερῶς δρωμένοις ὁ ἱεράρχης ἐμφαίνει, τὰ μὲν ἐγκεκαλυμμένα δῶρα πρὸς τὸ ἐμφανὲς ἄγων, τὸ δὲ ἐνιαῖον αὐτῶν εἰς πολλὰ διαιρῶν, καὶ τῇ τῶν διανενεμημένων πρὸς τὰ ἐν οἷς γίγνεται κατ' ἄκρον ἑνώσει, κοινωνοὺς αὐτῶν ἀποτελῶν τοὺς μετέχοντας......Μετασχὼν δὲ καὶ μεταδοὺς τῆς θεαρχικῆς κοινωνίας, εἰς εὐχαριστίαν ἱερὰν καταλήγει μετὰ παντὸς τοῦ τῆς ἐκκλησίας ἱεροῦ πληρώματος. Ἡ μετοχὴ γὰρ τῆς μεταδόσεως ἡγεῖται, καὶ τῆς μυστικῆς διανεμήσεως ἡ τῶν μυστηρίων μετάληψις. αὕτη γὰρ ἡ καθολικὴ τῶν θείων εὐκοσμία καὶ τάξις, πρῶτον ἐν μετουσίᾳ γινέσθαι καὶ ἀποπληρώσει τὸν ἱερὸν καθηγεμόνα τῶν δι' αὐτοῦ θεόθεν ἑτέροις δωρηθησομένων, οὕτω τε καὶ ἄλλοις μεταδοῦναι.—DIONYS. AREOP. De eccles. hierarch. c. 3. Op. Antw. 1634. Tom. I. pp. 284 and 299, 300.]

in their days. And will you yet continue to affirm that we have no colour or title in the scripture and fathers for the reproof of your private mass?

But ye will urge, after your manner, to have an express sentence, that forbiddeth the priest to receive without company. I answer, Christ's institution, the example of the apostles, the common use of the fathers was other ways; therefore the priest should not communicate without other. Ye have no express commandment that forbiddeth you to baptism in the name of the Father only, but that Christ's institution was otherwise. Will ye therefore say that ye may, without offence, baptize in the name of the Father only? If Christ's institution in baptism be a sufficient forbidding of the contrary to be used; why should not his words and manner used in the supper forbid you to do the contrary? Cyprian (as I have said) taketh it for a full prohibition of the contrary; and if you will not, ye must of necessity weaken his reasoning against those that he writeth: which did bring even as good reasons and as holy considerations for their part, as ye be able to devise any for yours. Now that I have in this manner laid the foundation of our proofs, I will proceed to examine the residue of your arguments against us.

CAP. IV.

In reciting the authority of Chrysostom, you bring in a similitude or comparison, which of how small force they be in proving, your learning cannot be so little but that ye must needs know. Even as (say you) it is to be wished that all contention and strife were clean banished, and yet men are not to be forbidden to sue for their right when they be injured; so is it to be wished that people were so devout, as they would daily receive their housel (for so ye term it): and yet is not the priest to be letted to receive, when the people will not dispose themselves unto it. Beside that ye conclude here only the case of necessity, (which helpeth the common use of your private mass very little,) ye make your comparison between things very unlike and of nature divers: that is, between possible and unpossible, and lawful and unlawful. That all contention should be banished from among men in this world is a thing unpossible, and a perfection not to be looked for in this frail life. But in a Christian congregation, to have some of the people or ministers to communicate orderly with the chief minister celebrating, is a thing so possible, as both the space of many hundred years it was continually used in the church, and may at this day with good example and instruction of the ministers be brought to pass, although not every day, yet very oftentimes. Moreover, to sue for one's right is not only a thing suffered, but of itself lawful and good: and we have thereof example and authority in God's word. But for the priest to minister the Lord's supper alone, is a thing neither tolerable nor lawful, but contrary to the form that Christ himself used, neither have we either autho-

A.

rity or example in the scripture as a sufficient warrant to alter that form that he used and appointed. Therefore your comparison is faulty on both parts: and especially for that ye seem to gather thereby, that it is no more necessary for company to receive with the priest, than it is to have all contention banished from christian men: which, as I have said, in the frailty of this world is unpossible. If such similitudes should be allowed, a man might break all God's commandments, and yet prove himself not to do amiss. Is not this a jolly reason think you? As it is to be wished that all variance and strife were clean abandoned from among christian men, and yet are not they to be forbidden to sue for their right, which be injured of other; so it is to be wished that all unmarried priests did live chaste; but if they cannot, the bishop must not forbid them to have a cousin of theirs to keep their house, with whom, *Si non caste, tamen caute*. This comparison is as rightly applied as yours is, and yet, how well it proveth, I will make yourself judge. All your drift in this part is, by alleging the corruption of the world and slackness of devotion, to signify, that the people cannot be brought to communicate with the priest; and therefore of necessity that he may receive alone. But, be the world never so corrupt, I think it as unpossible to have a priest to celebrate devoutly every day, as it is to have some of the people oftentimes to communicate with the priest. Wherefore I may as effectually conclude, upon the corruption of this time, that priests cannot be brought devoutly to mass every day, as ye do, that the people cannot dispose themselves, in this cold charity, godly to frequent the sacrament. And then were ye best to restrain your daily massing priests, and appoint them, either to once, or at least to fewer times in the year; as ye have taken order for the people generally to receive only at Easter.

But the priest (say you) is bound to offer up the daily sacrifice for himself and for the people. This is the root of all the abuses of the Lord's supper, that ye have brought into the church of Christ. This is it, wherewith ye do pitifully deface the death and passion of Christ, making yourselves, for your glory's sake, as it were means of reconciliation between God and his people. This is it, that hath discouraged christian people from the often use and frequentation of the sacrament. For hereby ye signify, that, of necessity, it appertaineth only to the priest, and (as you wrote before) the people to be left free to come as seldom as they will. This ye take for the ground of your reason in this place: and yet within few lines have twice rehearsed it without any proof at all. But indeed ye must of necessity leave that unproved that ye be not in anywise able to prove. For, sure I am, that neither the institution of Christ maketh mention of any oblation or sacrifice to be done by the minister, saving only the sacrifice of thanksgiving: nor yet the scripture appointeth any bounden duty for the priest more to use the sacrament than other godly and well-disposed

B.

christian men. What signification have you in the words that Christ used in ordaining the sacrament, or in the manner of his doing, that he then offered himself to his Father? He did that the next day after himself upon the cross, as St Paul saith, perfectly once for ever: neither doth he grant his privilege of the everlasting priesthood to any, but to himself. Therefore when your priests take upon them his office to offer sacrifice propitiatory, they go beyond their commission, and take more upon them than their duty, not without just reprehension of arrogancy and presumption. Christ's institution (as the Evangelists and St Paul setteth it forth) is a teaching that he gave to us his blessed body and blood: and not that we should offer it up to God the Father. He said, "Take, eat, do this in remembrance of me," he said not, "give, offer, and sacrifice for your sins." A sacrifice is a thing given to God: the sacrament was a thing given to us. Nothing therefore can be of nature more contrary than your sacrifice, and Christ's sacrament. Wherefore it must needs be, that ye sucked this error out of the phrases and fashions of speaking that the old fathers used, perverting the same to a far worse sense than ever they meant it.

[Heb. ix. 28; and see x. 10, 12, 14.]

For what causes the Lord's supper is called of the doctors a sacrifice.

1.

This thing more evidently to declare, it behoveth to consider, that the fathers upon divers occasions used to call the sacrament by the name of an oblation or sacrifice. First, Clemens Alexandrinus, Tertullian, Irenæus[1] and other make mention of a certain

[1 Τῶν ἄρτῳ καὶ ὕδατι κατὰ τὴν προσφορὰν, μὴ

oblation or offering that Christian people commonly used when they came together to celebrate the Lord's Supper. In this they offered up bread, wine, and victuals abundantly, not only to serve the Communion (as we had a shadow of late years in the holy loaf); but also that of the overplus thereof as well the ministers might have their finding, as poor people also be refreshed. Hereof partly it came to pass, (the example being taken first of the common people,) that the administration of the Sacrament, of this offering, was called an oblation. As in Irenæus, Lib. IV. cap. 32, "He taught us a new oblation of the new Testament; which the church taking of the apostles, offereth up to God in all the world[2]." But in other places after, as in the thirty-fourth chapter, he expoundeth himself, and signifieth that

κατὰ τὸν κανόνα τῆς ἐκκλησίας, χρωμένων αἱρέσεων.—CLEM. ALEX. Strom. Lib. I. §. 19. Op. ed. Potter. Oxon. 1715, p. 375, or ed. Sylburg. Col. 1688. p. 317.—Vobis autem nulla procedendi causa, nisi tetrica: aut imbecillis aliquis ex fratribus visitandus, aut *sacrificium offertur*, aut Dei verbum administratur, &c.—TERTULL. De cult. fem.c. xi. Op. ed. Semler. Tom. III. p. 52.—Similiter de stationum diebus, non putant plerique sacrificiorum orationibus interveniendum......Accepto corpore Domini et reservato, utrumque salvum est; et participatio sacrificii, et executio officii.—ID. De Oratione, c. xiv. ib. Tom. IV. p. 14, 15.—Novi Testamenti novam docuit oblationem, quam Ecclesia ab Apostolis accipiens, in universo mundo offert Deo, ei qui alimenta nobis præstat, &c.—IRENÆI Adv. Hæres. Lib. IV. c. 32. ed. Grab. Ox. 1702, p. 323.—Sacrificia et in Ecclesia......, Quoniam igitur cum simplicitate Ecclesia offert, juste munus ejus purum sacrificium apud Deum deputatum est.—ID. ib. c. 34, pp. 325, 6.]
[2 See the preceding note.]

he speaketh not of the offering of the Sacrament consecrated, but of the bread and wine offered: partly, to the use of the Supper; partly, to the finding of the poor. "It behoveth us," saith he, "to offer to God the first fruits of his creatures." And again a little after: "We must make offering up to God, and in all things be found thankful to God our Maker, offering up to Him the first fruits of his creatures, in pure mind, in faith without hypocrisy, in firm hope, in fervent love. And this pure offering the church only offereth to our Maker, giving to him part of his creatures with thanksgiving[1]." Justin also, in his Apology, affirmeth[2], that, after the communion, all that would offered to the behalf of poor people, fatherless children, and sick persons.

2. Another occasion that the doctors used those terms of sacrificing and offering was, that, in celebration of the Sacrament, they had prayer for all states, and thanksgiving to God for all his benefits: which the doctors

[1 Offerre igitur oportet Deo primitias ejus creaturæ......Oportet enim nos oblationem Deo facere, et in omnibus gratos inveniri fabricatori Deo, in sententia pura et fide sine hypocrisi, in spe firma, in dilectione ferventi, primitias earum quæ sunt ejus creaturarum offerentes. Hanc oblationem Ecclesia sola pura offert fabricatori, offerens ei cum gratiarum actione ex creatura ejus.—IREN. Adv. Hær. Lib. IV. c. 34. ed. cit. pp. 325, 326.]

[2 Οἱ εὐποροῦντες δὲ καὶ βουλόμενοι κατὰ προαίρεσιν ἕκαστος τὴν ἑαυτοῦ ὃ βούλεται δίδωσι, καὶ τό συλλεγόμενον παρὰ τῷ προεστῶτι ἀποτίθεται, καὶ αὐτὸς ἐπικουρεῖ ὀρφανοῖς τε καὶ χήραις, καὶ τοῖς διὰ νόσον ἢ δι' ἄλλην αἰτίαν λειπομένοις, καὶ τοῖς ἐν δεσμοῖς οὖσι, καὶ τοῖς παρεπιδήμοις οὖσι ξένοις, καὶ ἁπλῶς πᾶσι τοῖς ἐν χρείᾳ οὖσι κηδεμὼν γίνεται. JUST. MART. Apol. 1. §. 67. ed. cit. p. 160.]

in infinite places affirm to be the true and only sacrifice of the new Testament. Clemens Alexan. *Strom.* Lib. VII. "If God rejoiceth to be honoured, when as by nature he needeth nothing: not without good cause we honour him with prayers, and send up to him that most excellent and holy sacrifice[3]." And after, in process of writing, he giveth the same name to the reading and study of a godly man. Whereby it may appear, (as St Augustine also signifieth[4],) that the fathers called every good and godly action a sacrifice, were it private or common. And therefore their successors, by little and little, bent the same name unto the action and celebration of the sacrament: wherein most solemnly prayer and thanksgiving were offered. So writeth Irenæus, Lib. IV. cap. 34: "We offer to him not as one that needeth, but giving thanks for his benefits to us." And again, "He will have us to offer our gift to

[3] Εἰ δὲ τιμώμενον χαίρει [i.e. τὸ Θεῖον], φύσει ἀνενδεὲς ὑπάρχον, οὐκ ἀπεικότως ἡμεῖς δι' εὐχῆς τιμῶμεν τὸν Θεόν· καὶ ταύτην τὴν θυσίαν ἀρίστην καὶ ἁγιωτάτην μετὰ δικαιοσύνης ἀναπέμπομεν τῷ δικαιοτάτῳ λόγῳ γεραίροντες. CLEM. ALEX. Strom. Lib. VII. § 6. ed. Potter. p. 848. ed. Sylb. p. 717. He might have added a similar testimony from Tertullian. See his Treatise Adv. Judæos, c. 5. Op. ed. Semler, Tom. II. pp. 221—4.]

[4] The passage referred to is probably that in Augustine's treatise, De Civitate Dei, Lib. X. c. 6. Proinde verum sacrificium est omne opus, quod agitur, ut sancta societate inhæreamus Deo, relatum scilicet ad illum finem boni, quo veraciter beati esse possimus......Cum igitur vera sacrificia opera sint misericordiæ, sive in nos ipsos, sive in proximos, quæ referuntur ad Deum, &c.—AUGUST. Op. ed. Bened. Paris. Tom. VII. col. 242, 243.]

the altar oftentimes: our altar is in heaven, for thither our prayers and offerings be directed[1]." To this agreeth Eusebius *de demonstr. Evang.* Lib. I: "We offer," saith he, "to the most high God a sacrifice of praise: we offer a full, sweet, and holy sacrifice, after a new sort, according to the New Testament." And that ye may not object, that in this place he speaketh not of the sacrament, it followeth in this wise: "Let my prayer be made as incense in thy sight. Therefore we do sacrifice and burn incense to him: sometime celebrating the remembrance of that great sacrifice, according to the mysteries instituted by himself, both giving thanks to God for our salvation, and offering holy hymns and prayers unto him: sometime consecrating and bequeathing ourselves wholly to him both in body and mind[2]." Here he speaketh of the sa-

[[1] Offerimus autem ei, non quasi indigenti, sed gratias agentes Dominationi ejus....... Nos quoque offerre vult munus ad altare frequenter sine intermissione. Est ergo altare in cœlis (illuc enim preces nostræ et oblationes nostræ diriguntur) et templum.—IREN. Adv. Hær. Lib. IV. c. 34. ed. Grab. p. 328.]

[[2] Θύομεν δῆτα τοιγαροῦν τῷ ἐπὶ πάντων Θεῷ θυσίαν αἰνέσεως· θύομεν τὸ ἔνθεον, καὶ σεμνὸν, καὶ ἱεροπρεπὲς θῦμα· θύομεν καινῶς κατὰ τὴν καινὴν Διαθήκην τὴν καθαρὰν θυσίαν........Τοῦτό τοι καὶ ἄλλος διδάσκει προφήτης, ὁ φήσας, Γενηθήτω ἡ προσευχή μου ὡς θυμίαμα ἐνώπιόν σου. οὐκοῦν καὶ θύομεν, καὶ θυμιῶμεν· τοτὲ μὲν τὴν μνήμην τοῦ μεγάλου θύματος κατὰ τὰ πρὸς αὐτοῦ παραδοθέντα μυστήρια ἐπιτελοῦντες, καὶ τὴν ὑπὲρ σωτηρίας ἡμῶν εὐχαριστίαν δι' εὐσεβῶν ὕμνων τε καὶ εὐχῶν τῷ Θεῷ προσκομίζοντες· τοτὲ δὲ σφᾶς αὐτοὺς ὅλῳ καθιερoῦντες αὐτῷ, καὶ τῷ γε Ἀρχιερεῖ αὐτοῦ Λόγῳ, αὐτῷ σώματι καὶ ψυχῇ ἀνακείμενοι.—EUSEBII PAMPH. CÆS. Demonstr. Evangel. Lib. I. cap. ult. ed. Colon. 1688. fol. p. 40.]

crament and maketh no mention of any sacrifice propitiatory, but only of the sacrifice of remembrance by prayer and thanksgiving, and of the offering up of ourselves to God: which is the offering of Christ's "mystical body," that St Augustine speaketh of in divers places: of whose testimonies ye are wont to bring some for the confirmation of your sacrifice. As that he hath, *De civitate Dei*. "The sacrifice," saith he, " that we offer is Christ's body." But immediately he declareth, that he meant his mystical body, that is, the unity of the faithful congregation. For he addeth, "which we offer not to martyrs, because they be the same body themselves[3]." How the bishop or chief minister offereth up the people in the communion, he sheweth in his 59th *Epistle ad Paulinum*[4].

Another cause that the holy fathers call the sacrament an oblation or sacrifice is, because, according to Christ's ordinance, we celebrate the remembrance of his death and passion; which was the only true and perfect sacrifice. And so may ye perceive

3.

[3 Ipsum vero sacrificium corpus est Christi, quod non offertur ipsis, quia hoc sunt et ipsi.—AUGUST. De Civit. Dei, Lib. XXII. c. 9. Op. ed. Bened. Par. Tom. VII. col. 674.]

[4 Epist. 149, in the Benedictine edition. The passage referred to is, apparently, the following, in § 16:—Voventur autem omnia quæ offeruntur Deo, maxime sancti altaris oblatio, quo sacramento prædicatur nostrum illud votum maximum, quo nos vovimus in Christo esse mansuros, utique in compage corporis Christi. Cujus rei sacramentum est, quod unus panis, unum corpus multi sumus.—Op. Tom. II. col. 509.]

that Eusebius did take it in the place before recited. For he saith, "We sacrifice, celebrating the remembrance of that great sacrifice," &c. Chrysostom likewise, *Hom.* 17 *ad Ebreos*, after he hath in many words declared, that there is no more but one sacrifice once offered by Christ for ever, he addeth this: "Do not we then offer every day? yes, verily we offer, but doing it in remembrance of his death." And again, "That we do is done to the remembrance of that was done before[1]." St Augustine also *De fide ad Petrum*, declareth the same very plainly. "Believe stedfastly," saith he, "and in no ways doubt, that the only-begotten of God, being made flesh for us, did offer himself a sacrifice to God as a sweet savour. To whom with the Father and Holy Ghost in the old Testament beasts were offered: and to whom now, together with the Father and Holy Ghost, with whom he hath one divinity, the church ceaseth not to offer the sacrifice of bread and wine." He saith not of the body and blood of Christ. "For in those carnal sacrifices there was the figure of the flesh

[1 'Ημεῖς καθ' ἑκάστην ἡμέραν οὐ προσφέρομεν; προσφέρομεν μὲν, ἀλλ' ἀνάμνησιν ποιούμενοι τοῦ θανάτου αὐτοῦ......Ὁ ἀρχιερεὺς ἡμῶν ἐκεῖνός ἐστιν ὁ τὴν θυσίαν τὴν καθαίρουσαν ἡμᾶς προσενεγκών. ἐκείνην προσφέρομεν καὶ νῦν, τὴν τότε τε προσενεχθεῖσαν, τὴν ἀνάλωτον. τοῦτο εἰς ἀνάμνησιν γίνεται τοῦ τότε γενομένου. τοῦτο γὰρ ποιεῖτέ, φησιν, εἰς τὴν ἐμὴν ἀνάμνησιν. οὐκ ἄλλην θυσίαν, καθάπερ ὁ ἀρχιερεὺς τότε, ἀλλὰ τὴν αὐτὴν ἀεὶ ποιοῦμεν· μᾶλλον δὲ ἀνάμνησιν ἐργαζόμεθα θυσίας.— CHRYSOST. Comm. in Hebr. Hom. 17. § 3. Op. ed. Bened. Paris. Tom. XII. pp. 168, 169.]

of Christ, which, &c., but in this our sacrifice there is a thanksgiving and remembrance of the body and blood of Christ, that he gave and shed for us[2]." Here he saith not, there is an offering of the body and blood for our sins, which he would not have omitted, if the church had taught so in his time.

For some of these causes before rehearsed, the fathers used to call the Lord's supper a sacrifice: not meaning, as you do, that it was a sacrifice propitiatory to be offered of the priests for themselves and for the people. This your fashion of speaking ye seem to take of the manner of the Jewish priests, which had an offering for them and the people. As though Christ had left to

[[2] The treatise "De fide ad Petrum" is not by Augustine, but by Fulgentius. See the note of the Benedictines prefixed to the treatise, in their edition of it in the works of Augustine, and Cave's "Historia Literaria," *sub nom.* "Augustinus," &c. The passage is this :—Firmissime tene, et nullatenus dubites, ipsum unigenitum Deum Verbum carnem factum, se pro nobis obtulisse sacrificium et hostiam Deo in odorem suavitatis: cui cum Patre et Spiritu Sancto a Patriarchis et Prophetis et Sacerdotibus, tempore Veteris Testamenti, animalia sacrificabantur; et cui nunc, id est tempore Novi Testamenti, cum Patre et Spiritu Sancto, cum quibus illi est una divinitas, sacrificium panis et vini in fide et caritate sancta Catholica Ecclesia per universum orbem terræ offerre non cessat. In illis enim carnalibus victimis significatio fuit carnis Christi, quam pro peccatis nostris ipse sine peccato fuerat oblaturus, et sanguinis quem erat effusurus in remissionem peccatorum nostrorum: in isto autem sacrificio gratiarum actio atque commemoratio est carnis Christi, quam pro nobis obtulit, et sanguinis quem pro nobis idem Deus effudit.—Inter August. Op. ed. Bened. Paris. Tom. VI. Append. col. 30.]

us a like sacrifice as they had, daily to be repeated: whereas St Paul in his whole Epistle to the Hebrews reasoneth against it, and proveth the contrary, that Christ did it perfectly once for ever, in such sort, that it needeth not to be reiterated. But perhaps ye will object St Cyprian, where he, speaking of the dead, saith: "We offer sacrifice for them[1]." But it is evident he offered there for martyrs: which he was throughly persuaded were in heaven, and needed no offering for their sins. Likewise Ambrose mentioneth, that he offered for Valentinian the good Emperor[2]: of whom (in the oration made at his burial) he witnesseth, that he doubted not of his salvation, but believed, by the witness of angels, that he was carried to heaven[3]. Therefore their offering for the dead was no more but, as I mentioned before, the sacrifice of praise and thanksgiving to God for them. This thing the Greek Canon declareth more plainly: where it is mentioned, that they offered for the patriarchs, prophets, apostles, yea, and for

[1 Sacrificia pro eis semper, ut meministis, offerimus, quoties Martyrum passiones et dies anniversaria commemoratione celebramus.—CYPR. Ep. Presbyt. et Diac. &c. Ep. xxxix. ed. cit. Op. Pt. II. p. 77.]

[2 Date sacramenta cœlestia, animam nepotis nostris oblationibus prosequamur——Omnibus vos oblationibus frequentabo.—AMBROS. De obitu Valentiniani Consolatio. §§ 56 & 78. Op. ed. Ben. Paris. Tom. II. col. 1189 & 1194.]

[3 Nec nos quidem dubitemus de meritis Valentiniani, sed jam credamus vel testimoniis angelorum, quod, detersa labe peccati, ablutus ascendit, quem sua fides lavit, et petitio consecravit.—ID. ib. § 77. col. 1194.]

the blessed Virgin Mary the mother of God[1]: for whose sins it cannot be that they offered; which, by the testimony and faith of the whole church, be with God in heaven. This thing is well described by Chrysostom upon the 8 cap. of Matth. "Therefore," saith he, "the priest standing at the altar, when the sacrifice is proposed, commandeth us to offer thanks to God for the whole world, for them that be absent, for those that were before us, and for those that shall come after us[2]." The same Chrysostom also calleth this their offering *Rationalem cultum*[3], which ye cannot interpret a propitiatory sacrifice, but a reasonable worshipping of God by

[1 He refers here to what is called the Liturgy of St Chrysostom, which is used to this day in the Greek Church. The words, as given in the edition of this Liturgy published in the Benedictine edition of Chrysostom's works, are these:—"Ἔτι προσφέρομέν σοι τὴν λογικὴν ταύτην λατρείαν ὑπὲρ τῶν ἐν πίστει ἀναπαυομένων προπατόρων, πατέρων, πατριαρχῶν, προφητῶν, ἀποστόλων, κηρύκων, εὐαγγελιστῶν, μαρτύρων, ὁμολογητῶν, ἐγκρατευτῶν, καὶ παντὸς πνεύματος ἐν πίστει τετελειωμένου. (ἐκφώνως) ἐξαιρέτως τῆς παναγίας, ἀχράντου, ὑπερευλογημένης, ἐνδόξου δεσποίνης ἡμῶν, θεοτόκου καὶ ἀειπαρθένου Μαρίας.—CHRYS. Op. ed. Ben. Paris. Tom. XII. p. 792. This Liturgy, as now in use in the Greek Church, has the same words, except that for ἀναπαυομένων the reading is, ἀναπαυσαμένων. See the Ἀρχιερατικὸν, published by authority at Constantinople in 1820, fol. p. 7.]

[2 Διὸ δὴ καὶ ὁ ἱερεὺς ὑπὲρ τῆς οἰκουμένης, ὑπὲρ τῶν προτέρων, ὑπὲρ τῶν νῦν, ὑπὲρ τῶν γενηθέντων τῶν ἔμπροσθεν, ὑπὲρ τῶν μετὰ ταῦτα ἐσομένων εἰς ἡμᾶς εὐχαριστεῖν κελεύει, τῆς θυσίας προκειμένης ἐκείνης.—CHRYSOST. In Matth. c. 8. vv. 1—4. Hom. 25, § 3. Op. ed. Ben. Paris. Tom. VII. p. 311.]

[3 See the extract from Chrysostom's Liturgy, in the last note but one.]

prayer and thanksgiving for his holy saints:
by the which he hath builded his church,
and which now remain as members and
parts of his mystical body: whereunto we
also, by the celebration of the sacrament, be
joined, and so, as it were, knit in unity with
them. This was their offering for the dead,
and not a practice to pull souls out of purgatory for merchandise and money, as ye
have used in your private masses a great
number of years, to the great defacing of
the death and passion of Christ.

Wherefore your mass cannot justly be
called the Lord's supper, but a perverting of
the institution and ordinance, clean to another purpose and end than he willed to be
kept among his people. For the Lord's supper (as I said before) is a gift of God to us,
which we must receive with thanksgiving:
your sacrifice is a price to be paid to God,
and of him to be taken as a satisfaction.
The Lord's supper is a remembrance of
one perfect sacrifice, whereby we were once
sufficiently purged from sin, and continually
are revived by the same: your sacrifice is
a daily offering up of Christ for our sins: as
though it had not been perfectly done at the
first. The Lord's supper is to be distributed
in the common assembly of his people, to
teach us the communion whereby we all be
knit together in Christ Jesu: the use of
your sacrifice in private mass seemeth, by
the priest's sole receiving, to be a testimony
of separation, and a mean to bring the community out of christian men's minds. For,
after they once believed that priests must

sacrifice for them, they began to leave the communion and frequentation of the sacrament, as a thing either not appertaining, or very little appertaining to them, but especially to priests; and, by that means, the way was made to your common use of private mass. So much difference therefore as is between to give, and to receive; to remember one perfect sacrifice, and daily to reiterate a sacrifice; to celebrate in common as a testimony of unity, [and] to creep in corners or by-chapels as a sign of separation: so much difference is there between the sacrament by Christ appointed, and the sacrifice of the mass by you devised. This have I spoken more largely of this matter, than either I purposed, or you gave me occasion by any proof brought for the confirmation of your sacrifice. First, because this is another great abuse in your private mass, that ye take upon you to defend. Secondly, that I might declare the ground of your reason to be very weak, where ye affirm the priest to be bound of duty to sacrifice for himself and for the people. Thirdly, that I might answer more aptly to Chrysostom's authority, which next is to be examined.

The place of Chrysostom that you allege, is otherwise in him, than you recite it. For he saith: *Frustra habetur quotidiana oblatio, Frustra stamus ad altare: nemo est, qui simul participet.* "In vain we have our daily offering: in vain we stand at the altar: there is no man to communi-

CAP. V.

A.

cate with us[1]." As touching those words that ye most beat upon, "There is no man to communicate," by them to prove, that they received only at Easter, and, at other times, there were none at all to communicate with the ministers: I will shew you out of Chrysostom himself, that they must of necessity have another sense: and that in those words he useth that figure of aggravating, that he commonly useth in all places. For even in the same place, not many lines before the words that ye recite, he declareth that a number used to receive at certain other times. "I see many," saith he, "rashly, not passing how, and more of a custom than lawfully and of good consideration, to be partakers of Christ's body. 'If the holy time of Lent were at hand,' say they, 'if the day of Epiphany were come:' having no regard what he is, that is partaker of the mysteries. But the time of coming to it, the Epiphany, the holy season of Lent, doth not make them worthy that come; but the sincerity and purity of mind[2]." Do ye not here perceive, that many used ordinarily to come to the communion at the Epiphany, and in Lent,

D.

C.

An answer to Chrysostom.

[1 This passage has been already given in the note, p. 14. above.]
[2 Πολλοὺς ὁρῶ τοὺς σώματος τοῦ Χριστοῦ μετέχοντας ἁπλῶς, καὶ ὡς ἔτυχε, καὶ συνηθείᾳ μᾶλλον καὶ νόμῳ, ἢ λογισμῷ καὶ διανοίᾳ. ἂν ἐπιστῇ, φησιν, ὁ τῆς ἁγίας τεσσερακοστῆς καιρός, οἷος ἐὰν ᾖ τις, μετέχει τῶν μυστηρίων, ἂν ἐπιστῇ τῶν ἐπιφανίων ἡμέρα. καίτοι καιρὸς οὐ τοῦτο προσόδου. οὐ γὰρ ἐπιφάνια οὐδὲ τεσσερακοστὴ ποιεῖ ἀξίους τοῦ προσιέναι, ἀλλὰ ψυχῆς εἰλικρινεία καὶ καθαρότης.—CHRYSOST. In Ephes. c. 1. vv. 15—20. Hom. 3. § 4. Op. ed. cit. Tom. XI. p. 22.]

as well as he mentioned before at Easter? How can ye then gather by Chrysostom that there was no company to receive but only at Easter? But what if I declare out of Chrysostom, that some used to receive oftenertimes? will not your collection upon this place, that ye seem to triumph upon, appear to be of very small force? Hom. XVII. ad Hebræos. "Many," saith he, "take of this sacrifice once in the whole year, some twice, some oftenertimes[1]." Hereby it is most evident, that Chrysostom had other to communicate with him at divers other times beside Easter. The manner was (I grant) that some of custom addicted themselves to certain days. And in some places the bishops or synods appointed men to receive, once, twice, thrice, or four times in the year (as Augustine witnesseth[2]). *Concilium Eliberinum* appointeth to communicate thrice

[1 Πολλοὶ τῆς θυσίας ταύτης ἅπαξ μεταλαμβάνουσι τοῦ παντὸς ἐνιαυτοῦ, ἄλλοι δὲ δὶς, ἄλλοι δὲ πολλάκις.—CHRYSOST. In Hebr. c. x. vv. 24—26. Hom. 17, § 4. Op. ed. cit. Tom. XII. p. 169.]

[2 These words, "as Augustine witnesseth," ought, I conceive, to follow the words "certain days" in the preceding sentence; as there is no passage in Augustine, so far as I am aware, which speaks of bishops or synods appointing men to receive once, twice, thrice or four times in the year, while there is an express testimony for what is asserted in the preceding sentence, occurring in his Letter to Januarius, as follows:—Alii quotidie communicant corpori ac sanguini Domini, alii certis diebus accipiunt: alibi nullus dies prætermittitur quo non offeratur; alibi sabbato tantum et Dominico; alibi tantum Dominico. —AUG. Ep. 54. § 2. Op. ed. Ben. Par. Tom. II. col. 124. See also his treatise, In Johan. Evangel. Tract. 26. Tom. III. pt. 2. col. 500.]

in the year[1]. But these prescript times were ordained only for them that used seldom to come to the sacrament, that at the least, they should receive at those times, if they would acknowledge themselves to be of the church. Notwithstanding they did not only leave free to other to frequent the sacrament, but earnestly calleth them to it at every assembly of the people. As Ambrose grievously blameth the custom of many in the East parts, that used to come but once in the year: and saith, that he which is not meet to receive every day, will not be meet to receive once a year[2]. Therefore as in the primitive church very many in divers places used to be partakers of the sacrament but once, twice, or thrice, in the year, so it is evident, that divers other better disposed did receive with the bishop and

[[1] The canon here referred to is not considered to be a genuine canon of the Council of Eliberis or Elvira. The words of the canon that relate to the point here in question, as given by Gratian in his "Decree," are these:—Nec inter Catholicos connumerabitur, qui in istis videlicet temporibus, Pascha, Pentecoste, et Natali Domini non communicaverit.—Gratian. Decret. Pt. III. dist. 2. c. 21. in Corp. Jur. Can. ed. Col. Munat. 1783. Vol. I. col. 1170. On the question of the genuineness of the Canon, see the note of Mendoza in his edition of the Canons of this Council, published at Madrid in 1594, fol. under the title, *De Concilio Illiberitano Confirmando*, reprinted with additional notes, Lugduni, 1665, fol.]

[[2] Si quotidianus est panis, cur post annum illum sumis, quemadmodum Græci in Oriente facere consuerunt. Accipe quotidie, quod quotidie tibi prosit. Sic vive, ut quotidie merearis accipere. Qui non meretur quotidie accipere, non meretur post annum accipere.—AMBROS. De Sacram. Lib. V. c. 4. Op. ed. Ben. Paris. II. 378.]

ministers at sundry other times. That sort, because they were not so many as they should have been, and as Chrysostom wished for to have in his church, to exaggerate their slackness, he saith, "There is none to be partaker with us." Meaning that they were very few and seldom in comparison of that their duty was.

But if ye will stand upon these few syllables, *nemo est*, to prove that sometime the minister received alone; I answer, albeit this place did prove, that none of the common people would communicate, whose slackness he there reproveth, yet ye cannot by this testimony declare, that none of the ministers or the clergy received with him being bishop there. For the manner was not then, as you do use it now, that every priest received particularly at an altar by himself: but all the ministers and clergy did communicate together with the bishop or chief minister that celebrated. This to prove true, although I could bring in many examples and testimonies, yet I will content myself with one, that yourself putteth me in mind of, in reciting afterward the fourteenth canon of Nicene council; for therein order is taken by that holy council, that the deacons should not minister to the bishop and priests, nor receive before them, but after in order as it seemed more convenient[3]. Look for further declaration of this in examining the canon that ye afterward allege. Wherefore this your place of Chrysostom doth not sufficiently justify sole

[3] [See note p. 30, 31. above.]

receiving by one minister, as ye would have it seem to do, for proof of your private mass.

But if I should flatly deny, that the minister received, when none of the people were partakers, how could you prove it by this place? Ye will say, because he calleth it, *Quotidianam oblationem*, and the people, as appeareth, did not every day communicate. I answer, he named it *Oblationem*, either for that it was done in the remembrance of Christ's sacrifice, or for the offering up of the bread and wine to the celebration of the Lord's supper: he called it *Quotidianam*, to the imitation of the sacrifice of the old law: not because it was every day done without intermission, but for that it was oftentimes celebrated, that is, so often as the people assembled together to the church or common place of prayer, as he himself witnesseth upon the eighth chapter of Matthew[1]. At which times he always had, either some of the people, or the residue of the ministers and clergy to communicate with him, as the manner of that time was. But ye will here dally upon the proper signification of this word, *Quotidianam*, every day without intermission, every day daily sacrifice, every day mass, every day at the altar. Then must you give me leave as extremely to urge these two syllables *Frustra*, in vain is our oblation, in vain is our sacrificing, to no profit or commodity is our

[1 Τὰ φρικώδη μυστήρια........τὰ καθ' ἑκάστην τελούμενα λέγω σύναξιν, εὐχαριστία καλεῖται.— CHRYSOST. In Matth. c. 8. vv. 1—4. Hom. 25. § 3. Op. ed. cit. Tom. VII. p. 310.]

mass, in vain we stand at the altar, because it is done without company to receive with us. And surely, if a man rightly consider this place, he may justly marvel, why ye would allege it for private mass. For indeed there is nothing that hath any colour for it, but only the wrested argument that you wring out of the sound of these words, *Quotidiana oblatio,* and *Nemo est qui participet*: by the one part gathering, that the people then used to receive only at Easter, as they do now; by the other, that the priest received every day; and thereupon conclude your sole receiving. Which your collection, of how small effect it is, any man may perceive, if he consider these two things before declared: First, that at that time all the ministers received together, as it shall be afterward more plainly proved by your own testimonies: Secondly, that I have evidently shewed out of Chrysostom himself, that many used to receive at divers other times of the year beside Easter. For indeed he doth not there blame the general manner of all without exception, but of a number, that addicted themselves either to Easter or some other times, whether they were meet or unmeet: and at other common seasons would not frequent the sacrament, though they were more meet to receive. But these were not all (as I said), but a number of the common people: and the residue of the better disposed were so few, as oftentimes when the lessons of scripture were read, when prayers and thanksgiving were made, when bread and wine were (as the manner was) offered up for the communion, (which were the first parts of celebration, as appeareth in Justin[1],) then he was compelled either to suffer the ministers and clergy to receive alone, or else for lack of communicants to leave off the residue of the ministration. And that is it, that he complaineth of, and saith is done in vain: because it was imperfectly done. For the preparing to communion, the prayers and thanksgiving for that purpose, the offering up of bread and wine, the calling of the people to it, may seem to be in vain, when none did come to participate with the ministers. Wherefore Chrysostom in this place doth not only nothing confirm private mass, but also maketh very much against it: and declareth, that he took the right and true use of the Lord's supper to be, when the people were together partakers of the same. For if he had taken it as you do, for an offering up of the body of Christ for himself and the people; *or if he had at such times received alone, and thought it well done,* he neither could nor would have said, *Frustra habetur quotidiana oblatio*, "In vain we have our daily offering;" giving no other reason why it was vain, but because the people at such times did not receive. Therefore it appeareth by those words, both how necessary he esteemed the people's communion, and also that he took not *Oblationem* for a propitiatory sacrifice, as you do; for then he could not have said *frustra habetur*. To this purpose it maketh, that

[1 See note, p. 81. above.]

the same Chrysostom in the same place so earnestly calleth the people to it, as he saith to them: "Whosoever is not partaker of the mysteries, doth impudently and wickedly to stand there[2]." And in the 17. Homily upon the Epistle to the Hebrews he signifieth, that the manner then was, that a deacon stood in a place higher than other, and with a sign of his hands and a loud voice called the people to the communion[3]. This was not only at Easter, but at other times also. By this earnest manner of calling, therefore, it may appear how much this doctor took it to be of the substance of the sacrament, that a number should be partakers of it, and how far diverse his manner was from the fashion of your private mass. Now then your amplified conclusion, wherein ye claim Chrysostom to be wholly with you, sheweth itself to be very vain. And we may now as justly say, as we did before, that ye have no proof out of the ancient fathers for that ye do herein so earnestly defend; and that we have right good testimonies both out of the scripture and out of the doctors against it. For ye must not

[² Πᾶς γὰρ ὁ μὴ μετέχων τῶν μυστηρίων ἀναίσχυντος καὶ ἰταμῶς ἑστηκώς.—CHRYSOST. In Ephes. c. 1. vv. 15—20. Hom. 3. § 5. Op. ed. cit. xi. 23.]

[³ Διὰ τοῦτο καὶ ὁ διάκονος ἐπιφωνεῖ τότε τοὺς ἁγίους καλῶν.......Πλὴν ἀλλ' ἵνα μηδὲ τοῦτο ἔχῃς προφασίζεσθαι, τούτου χάριν μεγάλῃ τῇ φωνῇ, φρικτῇ τῇ βοῇ, καθάπερ τις κῆρυξ τὴν χεῖρα αἴρων εἰς τὸ ὕψος, ὑψηλὸς ἑστώς, πᾶσι κατάδηλος γέγονως, καὶ μέγα ἐπ' ἐκείνῃ τῇ φρικτῇ ἡσυχίᾳ ἀνακραυγάζων, τοὺς μὲν καλεῖ, τοὺς δὲ ἀπείργει ὁ ἱερεύς, κ.τ.λ.—CHRYSOST. In Hebr. c. 10. vv. 24—26. Homil. 17. §§ 4, 5. Op. ed. cit. Tom. XII. pp. 170, 171.]

use to ground doctrines upon the conjecture of a few syllables in one sentence, but compare the same with divers other places, as well of the same doctor as of other, and all together with the common use and manner of that time; and thereby gather a perfect conclusion. If you will scan and stay upon every word or clause in the doctors, as you do of the holy scriptures, and not consider them by conference with themselves and other, you may easily erect infinite new doctrines, that hitherto were never heard of in the church.

CAP. VI.

The reason that you bring in, grounded (as you say) upon our principal, is even of as much force as the other before mentioned.

A.

That is not evidently determined in scripture (say you) ought to stand as indifferent: but the necessity of company to receive with the priest is nowhere determined: ergo it ought to remain indifferent. Your second proposition is not true. For I say, and partly before have proved, that it is determined in Christ's institution. In Luke he

[Luke xxii. 17.]

saith, *Accipite hoc et dividite inter vos.* But how can it be taken at the minister's hands, and divided or distributed among them, unless there be a company? I see no sufficient warrant that ye can bring us for the discharge of this commandment. If ye will say *Dividite* is no commandment, but a counsel, that may be undone, and yet the substance of the sacrament remains: then belike ye will say, "Eat, drink," is no commandment: nor yet, "Do this in remembrance of me." But all be indifferent counsels that may be altered (as you after say) by spiritual governors. So that your spiritual governors may by this means clean alter Christ's institution: and leaving out "eating, drinking, distributing, doing in remembrance of Christ's death," (as they have done), devise a new fashion of their own brains, more fit for the church to use than that order which Christ hath left. But as he taketh away the right use of the sacrament, that taketh away from it, "eating, drinking, and doing in remembrance," &c. so I say that he taketh away the same that leaveth out "distributing." Which because it cannot be without company, I conclude the sacrament cannot be used in the celebration without company.

Cyprian teacheth you, that Christ's institution should be of more authority with you, than, so lightly, to change it at your own pleasure. Only Christ (saith he) is to be heard in the order of this sacrament. "And we must not in anywise depart from the precepts of the gospel. The apostle also more constantly and stoutly declareth in another place, that the disciples ought to observe and do the same things, that their master taught and did before them, saying in this wise: 'If either I or an angel from heaven teach you otherwise than I have taught you before, accursed be he.' Seeing therefore, neither the apostle himself, nor an angel from heaven, can tell us or teach us otherwise than that Christ hath once taught us already, and the apostle declared to us, I marvel how this came in use, to do contrary to that which Christ did[1]." And what, I pray you, can be more contrary, than, when Christ bade them drink, to take away the cup; and, when Christ bade them distribute among them, and St Paul willed one to tarry for another, until they came together, yet contrary to this (as you do) to minister and receive alone. Therefore I say with Cyprian, that in altering the sacrament, either by sole receiving or giving under one kind, ye worship God in vain with men's traditions. The matter that Cyprian wrote against, (that is,) using of water alone in the sacrament instead of wine, might perhaps, in case of necessity, be granted to some, that of nature could not abide wine. Nevertheless the necessity of a few is not to be drawn to a general example in the common use of the Lord's supper. Even so it may

[[1] Ab evangelicis autem præceptis omnino recedendum non esse, et eadem quæ magister docuit et fecit, discipulos quoque observare et facere debere, constantius et fortius alio in loco beatus Apostolus docet, dicens: Miror quod sic tam cito demutamini ab eo qui vos vocavit ad gratiam, ad aliud Evangelium, quod non est aliud, nisi sunt aliqui qui vos turbant, et volunt convertere Evangelium Christi. Sed licet nos aut Angelus de cœlo aliter annunciet, præterquam quod annunciavimus vobis, anathema sit. Sicut prædiximus, et nunc iterum dico: Si quis vobis annunciaverit præterquam quod accepistis, anathema sit. Cum ergo neque ipse Apostolus, neque angelus de cœlo annunciare possit aliter aut docere, præterquam quod semel Christus docuit, et apostoli ejus annunciaverunt; miror satis unde hoc usurpatum sit, ut contra Evangelicam et Apostolicam disciplinam quibusdam in locis aqua offeratur in Dominico calice, quæ sola Christi sanguinem non possit exprimere.—CYPR. Ep. ad Cæcil.; Ep. 63. Op. ed. cit. Pt. II. p. 152.]

be granted, that in cases of necessity one may receive alone: and yet that is not to be taken for a common manner and fashion in the church, when the sacrament is celebrated, as you used in the private mass.

That many circumstances of place, person, and time may be altered or taken away for good considerations, without impeachment to the right use of the sacraments, we grant you: but that company in receiving is one of those circumstances, that we cannot grant: as well for the reasons before declared, as also that we have no authority or example of the apostles or primitive church, that we may so do, as we have in all other things that you recite with more words than needeth. We dare minister in other places than Jewry, because we see in scripture that the apostles did so. We minister to women and laymen, because St Paul applieth Christ's institution to the whole congregation of Corinth, where were both laymen and women. We celebrate upon any day indifferently, because the apostles did so, *Actuum* 20. *uno die Sabbatorum.* We minister to fewer or more than twelve, by the example of the apostles in twentieth of the Acts, and of Paul in tenth and eleventh to the Corinthians. We receive in the morning, both because time is a thing indifferent in this sacrament, and also for that we have plain examples in the primitive church, without case of necessity or extraordinary chances. Christ said not, do it after supper, as he said, "Divide it among you." He did it after supper himself, because

B.

he would institute the sacrament of the
new law, in place of the sacrament of the
old law, that at the same supper he had
celebrated. Neither is it so much of the
substance of the sacrament to be done after
supper, as it is to be celebrated with
company; because of the signification of
unity and charity among christian men receiving together. Which is one chief point
in this sacrament of the Lord's supper.

The very proportion and likeness of that
ceremony of the old law, in place whereof
the Lord's supper is ordained, may teach us
the right use of it. The passover was a
solemn eating of the paschal lamb together
in remembrance of God's great benefit of
their deliverance and passing of his plague
from them. This ceremony they could
not solemnize alone; but if they had not
company of their own house, they should take
of their neighbours. Even in like manner
Christ, having finished at his last supper
the celebration of that ceremony of the passover, ordained for his even a like sacrament,
a supper, a feast, wherein they, being together, might celebrate the remembrance of
their redemption by his body and blood
given and shed for them. And even as the
Jews in solemnizing their sacrament had a
community of the remembrance of that
benefit, when their companies were in sundry houses separate, and yet might not one
alone eat the paschal lamb in his own house,
for that God had ordained it to be done with
company; so all the churches in the world
have community in the sacrament, be they

never so far asunder; and yet cannot any one alone minister it in one church without company to celebrate with him, because Christ's institution was otherwise. Will ye say here, that company to eat up the paschal lamb was not of the substance of the sacrament, but an ornament to commend it or set it forth, and might be altered by spiritual governors? Although the Jews were very bold in altering many ceremonies, yet we read not, that ever they durst alter this chief sacrament; as you take upon you to alter, change and take away, by your spiritual governors, all the parts of the Lord's supper; as I will declare to you in order, by the doctrine of this your defence of private mass.

The sacrament, as it is in use, hath two parts, the matter and the form. The matter is bread and the body, wine and the blood of Christ: the form of ministration is, that the minister should take the matter, and with the words of the gospel give it to them present, as Christ did. This form (say you) may be altered by your spiritual governors. For sometime the priest may receive alone without the people, sometime the people without the priest, sometime both together. So that no certain form of ministration is needful (as you say) in this sacrament to be kept. The matter also, ye signify, may be altered at your pleasure. For to receive the sacrament of the blood is not of the substance of Christ's institution. For, if it were, the church could not alter it, as you do commonly in ministering

to the people, and as you conjecture by
Tertullian and Cyprian, that they did in
the primitive church. Likewise the sacrament of the body is not so much of
the substance, but that upon considerations the church may commonly omit it,
and minister the wine only. For so you
seem to gather by the history of the child,
in Cyprian, to which the priest gave only
wine, as you say. So that the sacrament
of the Lord's supper, by your doctrine,
either hath no part, that is of the substance of it, but consisteth only of mutable
accidences, or else your church is of such
power, that it may clean alter and take
away Christ's institution. For if you have
considerations, for which ye may commonly leave out the wine, and use bread
only; and other considerations, for which
ye may omit bread, and use wine only;
when both those considerations come together, then may you take away both bread
and wine, and defraud the people of the
whole sacrament, or instead of that may
point [appoint] them another. What is
this but, with exceeding arrogancy, to make
your spiritual governors omnipotent in altering and transposing the sacraments by
Christ ordained? How much more comely
were it for you, revoking your error, to say
with Cyprian, "If we will walk in the
light of Christ (in the order of his sacraments), we must not swerve or depart from
his precepts and instructions; giving thanks
for that he, instructing us what we ought
to do hereafter, doth pardon us for that

offence, which by simplicity we have before committed[1]."

Where you endeavour to prove, that there may be communion in the sacrament, although it be received alone, in the one part you make your comparison (as you have done before) between things of nature very diverse; that is, between prayer and the Lord's supper. In the other, where ye confirm general communion between all saints, you prove that no man denieth. There may be communion in the benefit of prayer, say you, though one do pray alone; therefore in the Lord's supper also. Who seeth not, that prayer and the Lord's supper in the use of them be nothing like? That prayer is a common action, which, done of one alone, may stretch to the benefit and commodity of many, we have authority in the scripture, and example in Christ himself; but that the Lord's supper is such a common action, we neither have authority nor example in God's word. By as good a reason we may prove, that a man may baptize himself without a minister, because one may pray alone without one to guide him in the form of his prayer; or that one's baptism may profit another that is not baptized, as a man's prayer may profit him that prayeth not. But you must consider, that there is

CAP. VII.

A.

[1 Quare si in lumine Christi ambulare voluimus, a præceptis et monitis ejus non recedamus; agentes gratias, quod dum instruit in futurum quid facere debeamus, de præterito ignoscit quod simpliciter erravimus.—CYPR. Ep. ad Cæcil.; Ep. 63. Op. ed. cit. Pt. II. p. 157.]

great difference between the nature of sacraments, and other common good works. The sacraments have an external form by Christ appointed in the administration of them; which we may not alter. In other good works and godly exercises it is not so. And yet you reckon them up together, as though they were in all points like. As prayer, baptism, penance, confirmation, fasting, almsdeeds, &c. Another man's prayer or almsdeed may profit you, I grant, and procure God's grace for you. May another man's baptism therefore receive you into the church? or another man's penance satisfy for your sins? I think you will scant affirm it, although ye be ready to affirm strange things. No more therefore can your receiving profit another that receiveth not. Christ taught us, and his holy word commandeth us, to pray one for another. But he never said, receive the communion, or be baptized one for another.

B. To confirm your purpose, you bring an article of our creed; that is, "I believe the communion of saints." By this you prove, that there is a communion of all good things between them that are in place and time far distant; which we deny not. But to understand how little this communion of saints doth serve your purpose of sole receiving, it behoveth to consider what communion is. It is called of the Greeks, κοινωνία, and may be defined to be a society of a company or multitude, which, by certain laws and covenants, are all partakers of one thing. As among merchants, that upon certain conditions occupy jointly, and are partakers of like gain and damage, so all christian men have a certain society or conjunction; which consisteth in this, that they are all partakers of one salvation, and all members of one mystical body, the head whereof is Christ Jesu. The laws and covenants whereby we be all thus knit and joined together, are the word of God and the sacraments used according to Christ's institution. Therefore all churches of the world have the same word of God, and the same sacraments; and by them through faith are graffed into one and the same body of Christ, though they be thousands of miles asunder. By the word of God our faith is instructed; by baptism we be received first into the society of christian communion, and made members of the mystical body. By the Lord's supper we have from time to time heavenly food ministered unto us, and, as it were, lively spirit from the head of this body Jesu Christ. He therefore that is baptized in India, hath the same baptism that we have; and, being graffed into the same body, hath communion with us in baptism. Likewise they that receive the Lord's supper, be fed with the same food of the body and blood of Christ that we be; and so have communion with us in that sacrament, though in place they be far off. This is the communion between christian men; and this we most readily grant. But will you conclude hereupon, that there is like communion of the benefit of sole receiving in private mass, as there is of prayer, when a man prayeth alone? Then must ye say the same of baptism also. As for example, that our baptism here may benefit some that are in France, and receive them into the church; like as our prayer here may obtain the help and grace of God for them that be there. Which were great folly to affirm. Indeed we have communion in baptism; but every man's own baptism bringeth him the grace of that sacrament. And in like manner is it in the Lord's supper. We have all communion therein; and yet every man's own receiving doth profit him.

You will say perhaps, you do not infer this upon the argument of general communion, but only, that they which be in divers places, may communicate. Well, sir, I grant you that, but yet, ye should have inferred the other point, if ye would orderly prove that ye began. That is, to be like communion in the Lord's supper of one alone received, as there is in prayer, when one man in place alone prayeth for a multitude. The multitude that prayeth not, may have benefit by one man's prayer. But prove you by God's word, that one man's receiving or ministering the Lord's supper alone, doth benefit those that receive not, or that it is such a thing as may be done of one for many. And surely, it standeth you upon, substantially to prove that point, or else your private mass will fall to the ground, and be of no estimation. For if people shall understand, that your sole receiving in your mass doth not only nothing profit them that be present, but (as *Chrysostom witnesseth*) bringeth them in God's displeasure, if they receive not themselves, think you that the gain and advantage thereof will be so great as hath been before? Assure yourself it will not. But what do you infer upon this proof of communion between them that are in place far distant? Forsooth, in effect, this. That if there may be communion between those that are not together in one place, then a priest, saying mass in our lady chapel in Paul's at six o'clock in the morning, doth communicate with him that doth the like in Jesus church at nine of the clock the next day; although in place and time they be separate. Sir, I deny your argument, and say that neither the one nor the other doth communicate with any christian man, because neither of both receiveth according to Christ's institution. I confess there is communion between them that receive in sundry places according to the order by Christ appointed, as there is likewise in baptism. But, if they alter the sacrament, they do not communicate. I said a little before, that in the passover all the companies of the Jews in sundry houses did communicate, and yet one might not eat up the lamb alone, because God had taken another order. Likewise all societies of christian men communicate together in the Lord's supper, and yet should not one celebrate it alone, seeing Christ's example sheweth, and the apostle's interpretation declareth, that in ministering of it, there should be also a particular communion (as I may term it) between the members of one congregation.

Wherefore the granting of community between all christian men in use of the sacrament, doth make nothing against this, that Christ ordained it to be received as a feast with company; to the end it might more lively represent both the general giving and bestowing of his body to death for many, and also the unity and concord that ought to be between christian men receiving together of one loaf and one cup. For this purpose, as St Augustine signifieth, he used those external elements of bread and wine, to declare, that, as the bread of many grains is brought into one loaf, and the juice of many grapes is made wine in one cup, so the multitude of a christian congregation, receiving together the Lord's supper, are made members of one body, knit together in like faith and charity, and having like hope of salvation[1].

[1] Nihil hic de nostro afferamus; ipsum Apostolum identidem audiamus, qui cum de isto Sacramento loqueretur, ait, *Unus panis, unum corpus multi sumus:* intelligite et gaudete; unitas, veritas, pietas, caritas. *Unus panis:* quis est iste unus panis? *Unum corpus multi.* Recolite quia panis non fit de uno grano, sed de multis. Quando exorcizabamini, quasi molebamini. Quando baptizati estis, quasi conspersi estis. Quando Spiritus-Sancti ignem accepistis, quasi cocti estis. Estote quod videtis, et accipite quod estis. Hoc Apostolus de pane dixit. Jam de calice quid intelligeremus, etiam non dictum, satis ostendit. Sicut enim ut sit species visibilis panis, multa grana in unum consperguntur, tanquam illud fiat, quod de fidelibus ait scriptura sancta, *Erat illis anima una, et cor unum in Deum:* sic et de vino. Fratres, recolite unde fit vinum. Grana multa pendent ad bo-

The like effect is done in baptism, (as St Augustine witnesseth, *In sermone ad infantes*[2],) and we be graffed into Christ and made partakers of his body and blood. But he would have it more lively represented and set forth in this sacrament of communion, as well for the multitude as for the apt signification of the external elements. Moreover the ecclesiastical histories declare, when Chrysostom was banished, much against the people's hearts, that divers of them would not communicate with his successor, but had their assemblies and received the sacrament in another place by themselves, so that divers of them by the emperor's threatenings could not be constrained to communicate with him that was bishop after him[3]. This their doing was to no purpose, if diversity of time and place do

trum, sed liquor granorum in unitate confunditur. Ita et Dominus Christus nos significavit, nos ad se pertinere voluit, mysterium pacis et unitatis nostræ in sua mensa consecravit.—AUGUST. Serm. 272. Op. ed. Ben. Paris. Tom. v. col. 1104. Somewhat similar passages occur in Cyprian, Epist. ad Cæcil., Ep. 63; and Epist. ad Magn. Fil., Epist. 69. Op. Cypr. ed. cit. Pt. II. pp. 154 & 182.]

[2 The passage here referred to is not to be found in the works of Augustine, as now extant, but is given as an extract from Augustine's "Sermo ad infantes" by Bede, in his Comment. on 1 Cor. x., and repeated from Bede in Gratian's "Decree," Part III. dist. 4. c. 131. The words are these:—Nulli est aliquatenus ambigendum, tunc unumquemque fidelium corporis sanguinisque Dominici participem fieri, quando in baptismate membrum Christi efficitur.—Bed. Comment. in 1 Cor. x. ver. 16. Op. ed. Col. Agrip. 1612. Tom. VI. col. 365.]

[3 See SOZOMEN. Hist. Eccles. Lib. VIII. cc. 21 & 23. ed. Reading. Cant. 1720. p. 352, 3, & 355. Also SOCRAT. Hist. Eccl. Lib. VI. c. 18. ed. ead. p. 337.]

not declare a separation between them that be of one congregation.

The whole use of excommunication in the primitive church doth so sufficiently prove this, as no reasonable man needeth greatly to doubt it. The effect whereof this your device may seem to take away. For what other thing is excommunication, (as touching the external act,) than a debarring of the party to receive with other of the same congregation, and thereby to note him not to be of that mystical body. But after your device, a priest that is excommunicated of the bishop may say mass in his chamber, and affirm that he will communicate with him, whether he will or no. Because distinction of place maketh nothing to the purpose.

Because we necessarily require a number together, you press upon the matter very earnestly, and think by your dallying folly to drive us to many follies. For, you curiously require a measure of place, a prescription of time, and a certain number of persons: as it were thereby to portray unto you a perfect plat of a christian communion (for so it pleaseth you to dally in this weighty matter). I answer, that we see in the Evangelists and St Paul, that Christ took bread and gave with it his body; that he took wine also and gave with it his blood; that he did it in convenient place and time; that he had a company with him to receive, and willed them to distribute among them. Therefore (with St Cyprian) we count his example in these things necessary, and not to be altered. As for the kind of bread or wine, the fashion or quantity of place, the conveniency of time, the increasing or diminishing of the number or company, we reckon among those things that may be altered (as you say) by spiritual governors. But to appoint a geometrical measure of place, a prescript proportion of time, or one certain number, that may serve for all churches, times, and ages, is far above our reach. And therefore I leave it to be devised of such profound and curious brains as you and yours have; which, beside the word of God, and contrary to his working in his creatures, can comprise accidences without subjects, and bodies without fashion, quantity or measure, with other such high mysteries, which neither scripture nor any necessity of reason doth teach. For indeed our wits are so simple as, in God's mysteries, we can see no more than his holy word leadeth us unto.

Next is, that you burden us with Erasmus's authority, and challenge us that we will not believe his report. Sir, it seemeth very strange to me, that you, which have so much hated Erasmus, as ye have often chased him out of grammar schools, and driven him into the fire, should now in your need take help and succour at his hand. Truly we do now esteem Erasmus, as we have always, for a man of excellent learning, and a singular instrument provided of God to begin the reformation of his church in this latter time; and yet think we not all

CAP. VIII.

A.

Answer to Erasmus, Tertullian, Cyprian, and Cyril.

his opinions to be true. For you, I think, do esteem Tertullian and Origen, and that right worthily: and yet, if ye will grant all that they write to be true, I will prove you an heretic. Notwithstanding we deny not that which Erasmus saith in this matter, and knew whence he had his assertion before you told us. How little it serveth your purpose, I will shew hereafter. You confirm Erasmus' opinion with that Tertullian writeth in his second book *Ad uxorem*, of the Paynim's wife that was christened, and every day privily received the sacrament at home in her house. And also with the history that Cyprian rehearseth of the woman that unreverently opened the chest wherein she kept the Lord's body. To this also ye add Cyril's authority for reservation. Out of these places you suck not only sole receiving, but also ministering under one kind, reservation, yea, and real presence also.

Of sole receiving. B.

First, for sole receiving, it behoveth to consider, that in the time of Tertullian, Cyprian, and all that age, the church was in much trouble, vexation, and persecution: so that they could not have their ecclesiastical assemblies and congregations for common prayer and ministration of the sacraments so conveniently as afterward in time of peace. For every Paynim, especially if his wife, child, or servant, were turned to Christianity, was ready and sought occasion to bewray them, and bring them in trouble (as it may appear by the same book of Tertullian that you allege). Therefore they were oftentimes compelled of necessity to send the sacrament to such as were absent, and either durst not or might not conveniently come: as ye may perceive by Justin the Martyr that the fashion was in his time[1]. Hereof it came, that divers received alone in their houses. But neither these places, nor any other that you be able to allege, can prove, that there were ministers or priests privately celebrating, with other standing by that received not. That which these persons received at home was part of that [that] was distributed in the common celebration where company were; and, upon case of necessity, sent by the ministers to them being absent. But you should bring such places as might prove, that the common minister, in place of the Lord's supper, did celebrate and receive alone, other being present and not partaking. For such a sole receiving is your private mass that you pretend to strive for.

Now therefore let us see, how aptly your argument, gathered upon these places, doth conclude your purpose. Women and laymen sometime, in case of necessity, privately received at home part of that which was sent from the common celebration: therefore common ministers, as often as they list, out of necessity, may consecrate, and receive alone in the common place of prayer, when the people is present and doth not communicate. I think yourself may easily see of what force this collection is. That may be granted to

[1 JUST. MART. Apol. 1. §§ 65—67. Op. ed. Otto. Jen. 1847. 8vo. Tom. I. Pt. I. pp. 154—60. See the passages at length in p. 81 above.]

a lay person receiving, that may not to a priest ministering: that sometime in necessity, which may not always at pleasure: that at home where none is, that may not in the church where many be. Wherefore these testimonies are but weak grounds to build private mass upon.

You will, perchance, object, that such receiving in houses was used, when the church was in quiet and without persecution. I grant you (as the manner is) that fashions, brought in by necessity or some great consideration, be oftentimes kept and followed with abuse, when neither necessity doth constrain it, nor good consideration can maintain it: and so was it in this matter. Hierome against Jovinian mentioneth, that in his time some used to receive in their houses: but he earnestly inveigheth against that manner. "Why" (saith he) "do they not come into the church? Is Christ sometime abroad in the common place, sometime at home in the house?" &c.[1] In Socrates, the Second Book,

[1 The passage here referred to is not in Jerome's Treatise against Jovinian, but in his Letter to Pammachius in defence of that Treatise. It is as follows:—Scio Romæ hanc esse consuetudinem, ut fideles semper Christi corpus accipiant; quod nec reprehendo, nec probo. "Unusquisque enim in suo sensu abundat." (Rom. xiv.) Sed &c....quare non ingrediuntur ecclesias? An alius in publico, alius in domo Christus est? Quod in ecclesia non licet, nec domi licet.—HIERON. Epist. seu Lib. Apologet. ad Pammach. pro libr. contra Jovinian.; Epist. 48. §. 15. Op. ed. Vallars. Tom. I. col. 227. It will be observed that the translation given above is not quite correct. It ought to be, "Is Christ one person in public and another in a private house?" It must be added, that the meaning of Jerome in the passage

we read, that Synodus Gangrensis condemned Eustathius, for that, contrary to the ecclesiastical rules, he granted licence to communicate at home[2]. So that hereby it may appear, that a custom, that, in necessity, to some persons, is either tolerable, or *pius error*, is at another time and to other persons intolerable and *impia prophanatio*. If you diligently examine that manner of receiving in their houses at that time, which ye think to make with you, you shall well perceive it not a little to make against you. When they did celebrate, (as Justin before rehearsed doth witness,) they did not only distribute to them that were present, but, by the deacons, sent it to such as could not be present. Did they not in this point declare a necessity of partaking, if it were possible, at every ministration? Insomuch that when their place would not receive all, or other necessary cause did let them to come to the common place of prayer, yet, that they might be partakers of the Lord's supper, they sent it to them where they were. How well doth this fashion agree with your private mass! Wherein ye nei-

has been somewhat mistaken by our author. Jerome is blaming a custom of receiving the eucharist at home, at a time and under circumstances in which the party would have hesitated to receive it at church.]

[2 Εὐστάθιος μέντοι καὶ μετὰ ταῦτα ἐν τῇ δι' αὐτὸν γενομένῃ ἐν Γάγγραις τῆς Παφλαγονίας συνόδῳ κατεκρίθη, διότι μετὰ τὸ καθαιρεθῆναι αὐτὸν ἐν τῇ κατὰ Καισάρειαν συνόδῳ πολλὰ παρὰ τοὺς ἐκκλησιαστικοὺς τύπους ἔπραττεν...τὰς ἐκκλησίας ἐκτρεπομένους ἐπ' οἰκίας τὴν κοινωνίαν ποιεῖσθαι ἀνέπειθε.—SOCRAT. Hist. Eccles. Lib. II. c. 43. ed. Reading. Cant. 1720. pp. 158, 159.]

ther call, nor proffer, nor send to the people: but so do it all alone in sight of the whole congregation, as though it were a thing that nothing appertained unto them. Now then you may evidently see, that none of these authorities, hitherto alleged, doth prove directly your mass: that is, a sole receiving in the celebration of the sacrament.

But how necessary that time of the church did think it to be, that the people should be partakers with the priest, that Epistle signifieth that you attribute to Anacletus, where it is this [thus] written. *Peracta consecratione omnes communicent, qui noluerit ecclesiasticis carere liminibus. Sic enim apostoli statuerunt, et sancta Romana tenet ecclesia.* "After consecration" (saith he) "let all be partakers which will not be excommunicate. For so the Apostles decreed, and the holy church of Rome observed[1]." The same words by some are attributed to Calixte. Do you not hear excommunication threatened to all that do not communicate? Do you not hear, that the Apostles decreed it, and the holy church of Rome observed it? And will you yet stand so stubbornly in your assertion, that there was private mass in the primitive church? Will you have better witnesses of that time than Justin, than Dionysius, than Anacletus, than Calixte, than the other holy fathers before mentioned? Would Ambrose have

[[1] Peracta autem consecratione, omnes communicent, qui noluerit [noluerint] ecclesiasticis carere liminibus. Sic enim et Apostoli statuerunt, et sancta Romana tenet ecclesia.—ANACLETI PAP. Epist. 1. Concil. ed. Hardouin. Paris. 1715. Tom. I. col. 65.]

blamed the people for not resorting to the sacrament daily—would Chrysostom have said, that they which be present and not receive, do wickedly and impudently— would they have commonly used (as Justin saith) to send to those that could not be present,—if Christ's institution and the manner of the primitive church had been such, that the minister might celebrate alone without calling or offering, and people without offence be present and not communicate, as you of long time have used it? Surely, say what you will, and allege as oft as you list the authority of your holy mother the church of Rome so many hundred years, I think very few that have fear of God and care of their salvation, will give credit unto you; especially seeing you can bring no better testimonies for your purpose than in this defence you have used.

Another point that you pick out of these authorities of Tertullian and Cyprian, is for ministering under one kind: wherein we have the institution of Christ expressly against you, as we had in the other. For in the evangelists and St Paul we see testified, that Christ took bread and gave with it his body, and afterward took the cup and gave with it his blood, and willed them to observe and use the same. Here you must of necessity flee to your old place of refuge, that is, that to receive under both kinds is not of the substance of the sacrament, but such a thing as may be altered by spiritual governors. For Christ's body, say you, is not without his blood, and therefore he that

Against communion under one kind.

receiveth his body under form of bread, receiveth his blood also, *per concomitantiam*. Therefore you say, the people is not defrauded of that Christ's will was that they should receive; yea, and for good considerations and honourable to the blood of Christ, they receive it more convenient than under both kinds. O profound and deep-fetched reason, wherein you seem to make yourself wiser than Christ himself, that ordained the sacrament. While you will seem with your gay glosses to glorify the blood of Christ, you clean take away the right form and manner of his sacrament.

These are the vanities wherewith God justly doth punish you for your rashness in leaving his word and following the phantasies of your own brain. But it should have been your obedience to God's word to consider, that the communion of Christ's body and blood is not the work of nature in this sacrament. For, whatsoever is here given in these things, is to be taken by faith, and is offered to us in the words of Christ's promises. So much is given us as God appointed to give: of whose will and pleasure we know no more, than his words declare unto us. But Christ, as I said, took two parts of the sacrament; in one of the which, he said we should be partakers of his body; in the other, of his blood; and left his prescript and appointed words as well for the one as for the other. Wherefore we must more trust him than man's subtil device.

You allege a perpetual society of the

body and blood, which ye call *Concomitantiam*. It is your own device, and not Christ's promise in his sacrament. In Christ's natural body, that is in heaven, I know his flesh is not without his blood. But in the sacrament, which is no natural work, how will you assure me, that the flesh and blood is jointly signified and given to me under one part only; seeing Christ himself, who knew as well as you the joint condition of his flesh and blood, did notwithstanding, in two sundry external things, give the communion of them to his disciples? Therefore the faith of the communicants in the one part receiveth the body of Christ, trusting to Christ's promises: the same faith in the other part receiveth the blood, believing also our Saviour's words therein. It hath respect to Christ's words and promises; it looketh not how the body and blood is in Christ naturally. What ground shall our faith have if we leave the word of God? Oh, ye will say, our holy mother the church hath so ordained it. Yea, but I say to you, that if your mother the church of Rome be the fold of Christ, and if the sheep thereof be his sheep, they will hear his voice and obey his word. If they do not, allege the name as oft as ye will, I will say, you be sheep of another fold and not of his. For he saith, *Oves meæ vocem meam audiunt.* [Jo. x, 27.] He saith not, they hear themselves and their own devices, but, they hear my voice. Remember what Cyprian saith. Only Christ is to be heard in this. "And we must not look what other did before us, but what

Christ did before all other. When we doubt, we must have recourse to the order taken by Christ and by the apostles in their writing[1]."

But ye will say, the church hath authority to alter divers things, especially being indifferent, and not of the substance of the sacrament. Yea, but Cyprian saith, the precepts of this sacrament be *Grandia et Magna*. "And if he be called least in the kingdom of God, that altereth one of the least commandments, what shall be said of him that taketh away these great and weighty commandments[2]?" Cyprian wrote against those that were called *Aquarii*, waterdrinkers; which used only water instead of wine in the ministration of the sacrament. But they offended not so much as you do. For they altered only the liquor,

[[1] The former part of this passage is from Cyprian's Letter to Cæcilius, and the original has been already given in p. 62, above. The latter part, beginning, "when we doubt, &c.," does not occur in any part of that letter, nor do I recollect the *precise* words as occurring anywhere in Cyprian; but, no doubt, our author, quoting as he evidently did from recollection, had in his eye the famous passage in Cyprian's Letter to Pompeius:—Si in aliquo nutaverit et vacillaverit veritas, ad originem Dominicam et Evangelicam et Apostolicam traditionem revertamur; et inde surgat actus nostri ratio, unde et ordo et origo surrexit.—Cypr. Ep. ad Pompeium. Ep. 74. Op. ed. cit. pp. 215, 216.]

[[2] Sed et alio in loco ponit et dicit: Qui solverit unum ex mandatis istis minimis, et sic docuerit homines, minimus vocabitur in regno cœlorum. Quod si nec minima de mandatis Dominicis licet solvere, quanto magis tam magna, tam grandia, tam ad ipsum Dominicæ passionis et nostræ redemptionis sacramentum pertinentia, fas non est infringere.—Cypr. Ep. ad Cæcil. Ep. 63. Op. ed. cit. p. 155.]

and that upon holy considerations. They kept the words and promises of Christ. But you take away the one part clean, and leave out the words and most comfortable promises of Christ's blood to be shed for us. If then Cyprian were so earnest against those users of water instead of wine, how much more earnest would he have been against this manner, if it had been common in his time?

Here, those places that you recite may seem to help you, and to make against us. For, where Tertullian speaketh of the Paynim's wife, he mentioneth bread only. And when Cyprian reporteth that the woman kept the Lord's body in her coffer, it may seem to be under one kind. These are but conjectures, and the same very uncertain: for oftentimes in the doctors, where one kind is mentioned, both are understanded, as after shall more appear. But to make this more probable, you allege afterward out of Ambrose the history of *Satyrus* his brother, that hanged the sacrament about his neck in a stole, (as you call it,) when in a shipwreck he leaped into the sea: which must needs be in form of bread only, because neither our brain nor yours can devise which way wine can be in such an instrument inclosed. Surely if we had not known before, that you had nothing in the ancient Fathers directly to maintain your maiming of Christ's sacrament; this your conjectural gatherings and surmising reasons would most evidently declare it to be true. Would a man think, that any, having the fear of God, would, in so weighty matters, either ground his own conscience, or seek to confirm others by such feeble proofs and arguments? Is not this a strong reason, think you? *Satyrus* St Ambrose's brother, in extreme danger of shipwreck, purposing to leap into the sea, took of one that was in the ship only the sacrament of the Lord's body, and tied it about his neck: therefore in the primitive church, in ministration of the sacrament, they gave only one kind unto the laity. Though it had been here mentioned, that Satyrus had, in this extremity, received one kind alone, it had been no argument to prove, that it might orderly be used in the church. But (as Ambrose signifieth) this Satyrus at that time was but, as I might say, a novice in christian religion, not so far instructed in the faith, that he was as then admitted to the communion of the Lord's supper. And therefore he had not the sacrament about himself, but took it of other christian men that were there; which whether they were ministers or other, the place maketh no mention, but that it calleth them, *Initiatos*: that is, such as in the congregation were admitted to the communion. Neither is there anything to the contrary, but that the same persons, which had the sacrament of our Lord's body, had also about them the sacrament of the blood, either in some convenient vessel, or else after some other fashion, as divers of simplicity upon a zeal at that time used: that is, either by soaking the sacrament of the body in the wine, or else by moistening a linen cloth in the sacrament of the blood, and so carrying it with them.

For, even as I signified before, that persecution and trouble of the church at the beginning drave some to receive at home in their houses; in like manner the same troublous time, and other cases of necessity, with fervency of zeal, caused men to seek other shifts also, and to do those things by simplicity upon zeal at a time, that in the common use of the sacraments they could not do according to the word of God. Therefore as some learned and holy men for the time did wink and bear with such things, so afterward other, even as holy and profoundly learned, did mislike and reprove the same. As for example, when men did travel any dangerous journey, and for zeal and devotion would have the sacrament with them; because they could not conveniently carry wine with them, that they might go as nigh to Christ's institution as might be, they would soak the sacrament of our Lord's body in the blood. Some other would moisten a linen cloth in the sacrament of blood, (as I said before,) and keep it to moisten with water when they would receive. Some, that either of nature could not, or for religion would not drink wine, at other times, used only water. Some upon other considerations used milk for wine in the sacrament. Some were persuaded that in such cases men might use one kind. Wherefore to sick men or children they would use wine alone. But the particular cases of a few ought not to be taken for a general rule of the holy church. Neither those things which some did (as Cyprian termeth it) upon simplicity by sufferance, should be brought as testimonies what the church either then did, or ought now commonly to do. For a man may well doubt, whether these shifts that men in necessity did use beside the institution of Christ, were acceptable to God or no, although divers of them might seem to proceed of a fervent zeal, and to be done of good and godly men. It appeareth in Cyprian, that many of them that used water for wine, were godly men; and yet by zeal and simplicity did err. Therefore he saith of them in this manner: "If any of our predecessors, either by ignorance or simplicity, did not observe and keep that which the Lord by his example and instruction did teach us to do, by God's mercy his simplicity may be pardoned. But we cannot be forgiven, which be instructed and admonished by the Lord to do as he did, &c.[1]" The godly and holy Fathers did bear in many points with the zeal and simplicity of a number in that time. Wherefore those examples cannot be brought justly to prove the common manner used in the primitive church, which by manifest testimonies I will a little after declare to have been far otherwise in the same times that these things were done.

That the same things, before rehearsed,

[[1] Si quis de antecessoribus nostris, vel ignoranter, vel simpliciter, non hoc observavit et tenuit, quod nos Dominus facere exemplo et magisterio suo docuit, potest simplicitati ejus de indulgentia Domini venia concedi; nobis vero non poterit ignosci, qui nunc a Domino admoniti et instructi sumus, ut calicem Dominicum vino mixtum, secundum quod Dominus obtulit, offeramus.—CYPR. Ep. ad Cæcil. Ep. 63. Op. ed. cit. p. 156, 7.]

were not generally allowed, it may appear by this, that, when the church was settled, they did forbid those things, and bound them, so nigh as might be, to Christ's institution. Hereof ye have example in Julius his decrees, 1 *Hom. Conc.*, where all the fashions before recited are expressly forbidden. "We hear," saith he, "that some, fed with schismatical ambition, in the divine mysteries do consecrate milk for wine; some serve to the people the sacrament of the body moistened in the blood, as a perfect communion; others offer in the sacrament of the Lord's cup, the juice of grapes squeezed; some dip a linen cloth in the wine, and keep [it] all the year. Therefore," saith he, "henceforth it shall not be lawful for any in their sacrifice to offer any other thing, but only the cup mixed with water and wine[2]."

[*Hom.* is a misprint apparently for *Tom.*]

[[2] This is attributed to Pope Julius by Gratian, in his "Decree;" but Hardouin, in his edition of the Councils, says, " est ex Conc. Bracar. IV. cap. 1. anno 675" (Tom. I. col. 568); which is repeated by Coustant in his " Epistolæ Roman. Pontif." Paris. 1721. fol. col. 418. The words, as given by Gratian, are these :—Audivimus enim quosdam, schismatica ambitione detentos, contra divinos ordines et Apostolicas institutiones, lac pro vino in divinis sacrificiis dedicare : alios quoque intinctam Eucharistiam populis pro complemento communionis porrigere: quosdam etiam expressum vinum in sacramento Dominici calicis offerre : alios vero pannum lineum musto intinctum per totum annum reservare, et in tempore sacrificii partem ejus aqua lavare, et sic offerre. Quod quam sit Evangelicæ et Apostolicæ doctrinæ contrarium, &c.......Et ideo nulli deinceps licitum sit, aliud in sacrificiis divinis offerre, nisi juxta antiquorum sententiam Conciliorum institutionem, et calicem vino et aqua permistum.—Gratian. Decret. Pt. III. dist. 2. c. 7. Corp. Jur. Canon. ed. Col. Munat. 1783. Tom. I. col. 1166, 7.]

Gelasius also after him even as flatly forbade receiving under one kind; saying, "We find that some taking a portion of the Lord's body, refuse the cup; which, because I know not of what superstition they do it, either let them take the whole sacrament, or be kept from the whole. For the division of this mystery cannot be without great sacrilege[1]." Here you see, that Gelasius doth count it and call it sacrilege to receive under one kind; and your sort, contrary to this, affirm it to be heresy, if a man say the people should receive under both kinds of bread and wine. If you would rightly have proved your ministering to the laity in one kind, you should not have brought conjectures upon such rare chances as may seem for the time to be borne with, rather than allowed; but you should have shewed some plain and evident examples, that it was in the primitive church commonly used in celebration of the sacrament. But that you were never able to do, and so was it said in the protestation, that you call the challenge. For herein the whole number of the Fathers be against you.

And that you may not justly say, that we

[1 This passage also rests upon the authority of Gratian's "Decree," where it is attributed to Gelasius. It is as follows:—Comperimus autem, quod quidam, sumpta tantummodo corporis sacri portione, a calice sacri cruoris abstineant. Qui proculdubio (quoniam nescio qua superstitione docentur obstringi) aut integra sacramenta percipiant, aut ab integris arceantur: quia divisio unius ejusdemque mysterii sine grandi sacrilegio non potest provenire.—Gratian. Decret. Pt. III. dist. 2. c. 12. Corp. Jur. Can. ed. cit. Tom. I. col. 1168.]

brag of our empty boxes, that have the name only, and no stuff in them, I will rehearse and shew you some of the matter, which shall be directly applied to that malady and disease that you have brought to the right use of the Lord's holy sacrament. You heard before rehearsed out of Justin, declaring the manner of the church of Rome in his time, that both bread and wine were given to companies of the town and country, and the same also sent unto those that were absent. Here is manifestly declared, that such as were absent, and received at home in their houses, had both kinds sent unto them, contrary to your conjecture upon Tertullian, where, you say, one kind only is mentioned and therefore received. Tertullian and Justin were both of the church of Rome, and were not in time far asunder. Therefore it is like, one manner was used in both their ages. "The flesh," saith Tertullian himself, "is fed with the body and blood, that the soul may be filled of God[2]." He saith not only the body, wherein the blood also may be understanded, but he addeth separately the "Blood:" declaring the manner of Christ's sacrament ministered in two sundry parts. Cyprian also, speaking not only of priests, but of other laymen that were like to abide persecution and martyrdom for Christ, saith in this wise. "How do we teach and provoke them to shed their blood in confession of Christ, if we deny them his blood? or

B.

[2 Caro corpore et sanguine Christi vescitur, ut et anima de Deo saginetur.—TERTULL. De Resurr. Carnis. c. 8. Op. ed. cit. Tom. III. p. 176.]

how make we them meet for the cup of martyrdom, if we do not first by communion admit them to drink the cup of the Lord[1]?" Is not this a plain testimony what manner of ministration was used in Cyprian's time? And will you then, upon a surmise, gather the contrary? If ye read this father in all places where he speaketh of the sacrament, you shall find nothing more common than *Bibi sanguinem Christi*[2]. "How wilt thou," saith Ambrose to Theodosius the emperor, "with those hands receive the holy body of our Lord? how wilt thou be so bold with thy mouth to be partaker of the Lord's blood[3]?" This emperor was a layman; neither is it likely that he received any otherwise than the other people did at that time. And shall we think, by a vain conjecture of the history of Satyrus, that the

[1 Nam quo modo docemus aut provocamus eos in confessione nominis sanguinem suum fundere, si eis militaturis Christi sanguinem denegamus? aut quo modo ad martyrii poculum idoneos facimus, si non eos prius ad bibendum in ecclesia poculum Domini jure communicationis admittimus?—CYPR. et alior. Ep. ad Cornel. Ep. 57. inter Op. Cypr. ed. cit. Pt. II. p. 117.]
[2 As for instance,—Se quotidie calicem sanguinis Christi bibere.—CYPR. Ep. ad Pleb. Thibar. Ep. 58. Op. Cypr. ed. cit. Pt. II. p. 112.]
[3 These words are taken from Theodoret's account of Ambrose's address to Theodosius, on his entering the church at Milan, after the slaughter that took place under his orders at Thessalonica. The words as given by Theodoret are as follows:— Πῶς δὲ τοιαύταις ὑποδέξῃ χερσὶ τοῦ Δεσπότου τὸ πανάγιον σῶμα; πῶς δὲ τῷ στόματι προσοίσεις τὸ αἷμα τὸ τίμιον;—THEODORET. Hist. Eccles. Lib. v. c. 17. Op. ed. Noesselt. Halæ, 1771. Tom. III. pp. 1046, 7.]

custom of that time was otherwise, because your mocking head could not devise how to carry wine in a stole? And yet they of that time (as ye may perceive by dipping a linen cloth in the sacrament of the blood) had devised which way it might be done. But to our purpose. "Without confusion and doubt," saith Gregory Nazianzene, "eat his body and drink his blood, if thou have any desire of life in thee[4]." And yet he speaketh to the people, *Oratione* 4, *in Sanctum Pascha.* Hilarius also, *lib.* 8, *De Trinitate.* "These things," saith he, "being eaten and drunk make that we be in Christ and Christ in us[5]." Basil, *De Baptismo*, upon these words, "As often as ye shall eat," &c. "What profit have those words?" saith he. "That we, eating and drinking, may be perpetually mindful of him that died for us; and so may be instructed in the sight of God and his Christ, of necessity to keep the doctrine delivered by his apostles[6]." Here, beside the mention both

[4] Ἀλλ' ἀνεπαισχύντως καὶ ἀνενδοιάστως φάγε τὸ σῶμα, πίε τὸ αἷμα, εἰ τῆς ζωῆς ἐπιθυμητικῶς ἔχεις.—GREGOR. NAZIANZ. Orat. in Sanctum Pascha. Orat. 45. § 19. Op. ed. Ben. Paris. 1778. Vol. I. p. 860.]

[5] Hæc [i. e. caro et sanguis] accepta atque hausta id efficiunt, ut et nos in Christo, et Christus in nobis sit.—HILAR. De Trinit. Lib. 8. § 14. Op. ed. Ben. Paris. 1693. col. 956.]

[6] Τί οὖν ὠφελεῖ τὰ ῥήματα ταῦτα; "Ἵνα ἐσθίοντές τε καὶ πίνοντες ἀεὶ μνημονεύωμεν τοῦ ὑπὲρ ἡμῶν ἀποθανόντος καὶ ἐγερθέντος, καὶ οὕτω παιδευθῶμεν ἀναγκαίως φυλάξαι ἐνώπιον Θεοῦ καὶ τοῦ Χριστοῦ αὐτοῦ τὸ δόγμα τὸ ὑπὸ τοῦ ἀποστόλου παραδεδομένον ἐν τῷ εἰπεῖν· Ἡ γὰρ ἀγάπη τοῦ Χριστοῦ συνέχει ἡμᾶς, κ.τ.λ.—BASIL. De Bapt. Lib.

E.

of "eating and drinking," he addeth, "of necessity to keep this doctrine" of the Lord's supper; which you, in many points, without prick of conscience take upon you to alter. " Priests," saith St Hierome, upon *Sophon.*, " which make the sacrament, and distribute the blood of the Lord unto the people[1]." This man was priest in Rome in Ambrose's time; and yet he signifieth, that the manner then was to minister "the blood to the people." And shall the history of Satyrus, nothing pertaining to the matter, persuade us the contrary? What can be more plain and expressly against you than that Chrysostom hath *Hom.* 18, *in poster. ad Corinth.?* There he saith, that in this sacrament the priest's part is not better than the people's. " For it is not," saith he, " as it was in the old law, where the priests had part and the people part; neither could the people be partaker of that was the priests'. But now it is not so, for one body and one cup is indifferently offered to all[2]." And it is notable that he saith, " All be like worthy to be partakers, neither doth the inferior differ

---

1. c. 3. § 2. Op. ed. Ben. Paris. Tom. II. p. 650. The work is considered by the Benedictines as wrongly ascribed to Basil.]

[1 Sacerdotes quoque qui Eucharistiæ serviunt, et sanguinem Domini populis ejus dividunt.—HIERON. Comment. in Sophon. cap. 3. vv. 1—7. Op. ed. cit. Tom. VI. col. 718.]

[2 Οὐ καθάπερ ἐπὶ τῆς παλαιᾶς, τὰ μὲν ὁ ἱερεὺς ἤσθιε, τὰ δὲ ὁ ἀρχόμενος· καὶ θέμις οὐκ ἦν τῷ λαῷ μετέχειν ὧν μετεῖχεν ὁ ἱερεύς. ἀλλ' οὐ νῦν· ἀλλὰ πᾶσιν ἓν σῶμα πρόκειται, καὶ ποτήριον ἕν.—CHRYS. In Ep. 2. ad Cor. Homil. 18. in c. viii. v. 16. Op. ed. cit. Tom. X. p. 568.]

anything at all from the priest in that matter[3]. Why do you then (so plainly against Chrysostom) make difference of dignity between the priest and the people? Is not this, which Chrysostom speaketh against, one of the chiefest reasons that you have for the giving of one kind to the people? But St Paul, to Timothy and Titus, declareth other causes that should make the order of ministry honourable; and not to defraud the people of one part of the sacrament. Cyprian again, in the same sermon *De Lapsis,* that you afterward allege, and the same history, sheweth, that all the company of laymen and women took the sacrament of the Lord's cup and drank of it in order, one after another[4].

But I fear I shall seem to most men to commit much folly, in that I stand so long with authorities to prove that thing, which of itself is most manifest; that is, that in the primitive church the only manner, in the common celebration of the sacrament, was, that all received under both kinds of bread and wine. Seeing, therefore, Justin saith, that on Sundays bread and wine consecrated were distributed to companies of the town and country; seeing Gelasius calleth it sacrilege to divide the sacrament;

[3] "Ἔστι δὲ ὅπου οὐδὲ διέστηκεν ὁ ἱερεὺς τοῦ ἀρχομένου· οἷον, ὅταν ἀπολαύειν δέῃ τῶν φρικτῶν μυστηρίων. ὁμοίως γὰρ πάντες ἀξιούμεθα τῶν αὐτῶν.—Id. ib. These words immediately precede those just quoted.]

[4 Alluding to the words—Ubi vero solennibus adimpletis calicem diaconus offerre præsentibus cœpit, et accipientibus ceteris locus ejus advenit—occurring in the extract given above, p. 33, from Cyprian's Treatise, *De Lapsis.*]

seeing Cyprian counselleth that laymen should be admitted to the communion of the Lord's cup, and by a history sheweth that in his time they used it; seeing Chrysostom affirmeth no difference to be between the priest and the people in use of this sacrament; seeing all the residue of the Fathers of all countries and all ages of the primitive church agree to the same,—were it not more than wilful blindness not to see, that holy men at that time in celebration of the sacrament ministered both parts to the people, according to Christ's institution and the doctrine of St Paul to the Corinthians? Were it not almost desperate stubbornness to persuade the contrary to ignorant people, and by libels privily spread to detain the unlearned in error? But it stood you upon to say somewhat, lest you should seem to have nothing to say. And yet in very deed it had been better for the confirmation of your doctrine to have said nothing: for then perhaps such as of simplicity depend upon your authorities, would have thought, that you had had far better provision for your defence in so weighty matters; which now, seeing your slender and feeble grounds, will begin, I doubt not, as they have the fear of God, to mistrust your dealing, and more diligently examine the residue of your doctrine. It is not good for them any longer to walk on other men's feet, nor to be guided by other men's eyes, but themselves to see what way they go; lest their guides, either by ignorance or wilfulness, lead them into the pit of continual error.

The third point that you gather out of these testimonies, is reservation of the sacrament; which to deny (say you) is extreme impudency. I think you have not met with any, which have flatly denied, that in the primitive church divers used reservation. But it followeth not thereupon, but that a man may deny without any impudency at all, either that we have any testimony in the word of God to justify it, or, that all the holy Fathers did approve it. Or if ye will say the contrary, I will not doubt to make the crime of impudency that you charge us withal, to rebound upon yourself. But you will say, you have witness that it was used, and that of good men, which is sufficient. Indeed it is sufficient to shew, that it was then used; but it is not sufficient to prove, that it must therefore be always used; or, that all did well at that time in using of it.

Oh, ye will say, this is your old manner: so long as the Fathers make with you, you will admit them; if they seem to be anything against you, ye will reject their authority. Because you commonly take hold here, and through this odious report often use to stir men's stomachs against us; before I answer your reservation, I will protest what authority we attribute unto the old Fathers. This will I do, not with my own words, but St Augustine's in his epistle to Hierome: "I confess that I have learned to attribute this reverence and honour only to the canonical scriptures, to believe stedfastly without controversy all

that is written in them. As for other, I so read them, that, be they never so excellent in great holiness and learning, I do not therefore count it true, because they were of that opinion; but because they could persuade me, either by Scripture or good reason, that it was not against the truth[1]."
Here you may object, that men of such learning, holiness, and devotion, would never have written any such thing, if they had not thought it to be agreeable with God's word. Yea sir, I think they, as good men, were so persuaded; but that they did leave in writing many things, not only beside the word of God, but also against it, I think it is not unknown to you. And that other also may know it, and thereby hold us excused, when we do not in all points agree unto them, I will recite some proofs thereof. Clemens Alexandrinus with Justin and divers other taught, that Angels fell from their estate for the carnal love of earthly women: which doctrine, I think, you will not say riseth of true interpretation of the Scripture. The same Clement, *Strom.* 2 and 6, writeth, that men's souls are transformed into angels, and first learn a thousand years of other angels; afterward teaching other new

[1] Ego enim fateor caritati tuæ, solis eis scripturarum libris, qui jam canonici appellantur, didici hunc timorem honoremque deferre, ut nullum eorum auctorem scribendo aliquid errasse firmissime credam.... Alios autem ita lego, ut quantalibet sanctitate doctrinaque præpolleant, non ideo verum putem, quia ipsi ita senserunt, sed quia mihi vel per illos auctores canonicos, vel probabili ratione, quod a vero non abhorreat, persuadere potuerunt.—August. Ep. ad Hieron. Ep. 82. (al. 19.) Op. ed. Ben. Paris. Tom. ii. col. 190.]

transformed angels, at the length become archangels: which cannot be soundly taken out of the Scriptures. Justin, Lactantius, Irenæus and other wrote, that good men, after the resurrection, should live a thousand years in all joy, before Christ should come to judgment. And yet is that but a misunderstanding of the Scripture. Tertullian seemeth to attribute a bodily substance to God, and in divers places, *De Trinitate*, speaketh dangerously of Christ; for which, and like things, many would have had his works counted *Apocrypha*. Therefore he doth not always agree with Scripture. Cyprian would have heretics to be rebaptized, and speaketh so dangerously of them that are fallen from the faith, that he might seem to give some occasion to Novatian's heresy. What shall we say of Origen, in whom be found so many perilous doctrines, as both I in this place am loath to rehearse them, and in the primitive church divers great learned men would have had his books burned for the same? I could say the like of divers other, but that I fear some will maliciously gather, that I rehearse these things of purpose, so much as in me lieth, to deface the authority of the holy Fathers: which, God is my witness, I mean not; but only to signify, that, when we measure their doctrine by God's words, or teach not in all points as they did, we be not so much to be blamed as that men should count us, as you do, to control the doctors, and as it were to set them to school. For if God hath suffered them to err in so weighty matters as is before mentioned, (although for good cause I have omitted the greatest,) it may be also, that they have taught amiss in some other lighter things, and therefore are to be read with judgment, as Augustine counselleth both in himself and in other. Notwithstanding we do greatly esteem the Fathers; not only as holy men endued with singular grace of God, but also as right good witnesses and strong defenders of the chief articles of our faith, at that time, when Satan endeavoured, partly by cruelty of persecution, partly by infinite numbers of heresies, to deface and extinguish the same. Therefore who doth not much honour them, and (when truth constraineth) with reverence go from their opinion, is scantly worthy the name of a Christian man. Nevertheless, I think not the contrary, but if they had seen what abuses and superstitions would have followed upon divers things that they either taught, or for the state of that time winked at and suffered, undoubtedly they would either have recanted those things, as Augustine did many, or else would have made a more perfect interpretation of their minds. Before the Pelagians' heresy began to be spread, St Augustine so wrote of freewill, as he seemed not to himself afterward, sufficiently and as the truth required, to express the mere grace of God. Therefore, upon occasion of that heresy, he writeth more perfectly of that and of predestination, than either the other doctors do, or than it is to be thought that himself would have done, if that occasion had not been. So doubtless both he and many other would have done of divers things now in controversy, if at that time they had been brought in question. This much by the way have I spoken of my opinion in the doctors, so much as I can, to eschew the malicious report that your sort is most ready to spread of us in this matter.

Now I will return to reservation. We deny not (as I said), that some in that time did use it, as it appeareth by your witness of Cyril. As touching whose words by you in this place recited, I have this much to say,—that, as I know the same place is alleged of divers other, and therefore I will not plainly deny it, so, because that work of Cyril is not extant, I have good cause to suspect it. And so much the more, for that divers of your sort have alleged out of the same doctor in his work *Thesaurus*, certain words for the supremacy of the bishop of Rome, which are not there to be found. This unjust fathering of your own late devised fantasies upon the ancient doctors and writers of the church, may cause us justly to suspect the residue of your doing. But be it so, that those are Cyril's own words indeed. We have for that one suspected place a number of sound testimonies, that all did not allow reservation, nor think it according to the word of God. Origen upon the v. chap. of Leviticus. "The Lord," saith he, "deferred not the bread that he gave to his disciples; saying, take and eat; neither commanded it to be kept until the morrow[1]."

[1 The passage occurs in his comment (*not* on

Of reservation.

D.

The residue of his words upon the same place be such, as he seemeth thereupon to gather an argument, that it should not be reserved. He that wrote the sermon *De cœna Domini* in Cyprian, saith plainly of the sacrament, *Recipitur non includitur.* "It is received, it is not inclosed or shut up[1]." Isychius upon *Leviticum* at large declareth, how that in his time, if the ministers and people were not able to eat up so much as was consecrated, the residue was burned, and consumed by fire, that it might not be kept until the next day[2]. Therefore you may not force upon us to receive reservation, as a thing either grounded in Scripture or generally allowed by the primitive church. What will you say to your second

Levit. v. but) on Levit. vii. 15; and is as follows:—
Nam et Dominus panem, quem discipulis dabat, et dicebat eis, *accipite et manducate*, non distulit, nec servari jussit in crastinum.—ORIG. In Levit. Hom. 5. § 8. Op. ed. Delarue, Paris. 1733. Tom. II. p. 211.]

[1 Universa ecclesia ad has epulas invitatur. Æqua omnibus portio datur: integer erogatur, distributus non demembratur: incorporatur, non injuriatur: recipitur, non includitur: cum infirmis habitans non infirmatur, &c.—ARNOLD. CARNOT. De Card. Oper. Christi, c. De cœna Domini. apud CYPR. Op. ed. cit. Append. p. 42.]

[2 Sed hoc quod reliquum est de carnibus et panibus, in igne incendi præcepit. Quod nunc videmus etiam sensibiliter in ecclesia fieri, ignique tradi quæcunque remanere contigerit inconsumpta, non omnino ea quæ una die, vel duabus, aut multis servata sunt: sicut enim apparet, non hoc legislator præcepit; sed quod reliquum est, incendi jubet. Dies autem non commemoravit, ut quæcunque cujuscunque rei causa emergente remanserint inconsumpta, sive tempus in causa sit, sive quid aliud fuerit, ignis opus et consumptio fiat.—ISYCH. In Levit. Lib. II. In cap. viii. vers. 31. Ed. Basil. 1527. fol. 49. D.]

epistle of Clement bishop of Rome? "Let so many holy loaves," saith he, "be offered upon the altar, as may be sufficiently for the people. If so be any shall remain, let them not be kept until the morrow, but, with fear and trembling, let the ministers eat it up [3]." This was a bishop of Rome, this was Peter's successor, this was (as you say) head of the church; and yet you hear his appointment and order taken expressly against reservation. If ye will not believe us, why do you not believe your own? Will you say, with your testimony of Cyril, that Origen was mad, that Isychius was mad? Or if ye be not afraid to say it of them, will you say that Clement was mad? Well sir, if ye will prove us impudent or mad for not receiving reservation, I trust you see, that we shall have company in our impudency and madness.

But Clement's epistle presseth you hard in sole receiving and private mass also, and signifieth that all the ministers received together with the people. For, in the words before rehearsed, he speaketh of the mass that was used, when that epistle was made; and yet it willeth you to prepare for the people. Why do you not follow his authority in these points? You will

[[3] This is taken from a passage ascribed to Clement's second Epistle in Gratian's Decree, where we find the following words:—Tanta in altario certe holocausta offerantur, quanta populo sufficere debeant. Quod si remanserint, in crastinum non reserventur, sed, cum timore et tremore, clericorum diligentia consumantur.—Gratian. Decret. P. 3. De Consecr. Dist. 2. c. 23. Corp. Jur. Can. ed. Col. Munat. 1783. Tom. I. col. 1171.]

say, as you said in the beginning, if the people be absent, and, when the sacrament is prepared, either will not or cannot come to receive, Clement then sayeth not, that the priest consecrating should forbear, because the other bidden guests will not come. The church (you will say) did alway profess a communion, if any would dispose themselves. I answer: First, if Clement bade you prepare for the people, why do you contemn his canon, and on the holy day, when a number be present, neither call them, nor prepare for them. If the church always professed a communion, why have you one priest standing at the altar alone, with one singing cake for himself, which he sheweth to the people, to be seen and honoured, and not to be eaten? Where have you authority or example for that? Have you that in the Scripture? Have you that in the doctors? Have you that in the ancient councils? If you have, shew it us, and we will, without any more resistance, give over to you. If you have not, dread the wrath of God, for giving the occasion of so much ill to the simple people. Secondly, if the people will not come, when the sacrament is prepared, the priest alone ought not to communicate. For Paul willed the Corinthians to tarry one for another, and not every man to presume to eat his own supper, as I said before. Then, (say you,) if the people will never receive, nor the priest shall ever receive, by occasion of the people's slackness. As I have repeated once or twice before, so I say now again; that, to prove your case of necessity, you imagine such an impossibility, as cannot lightly happen among a christian congregation rightly instructed. So that, if some of the people will not at convenient times receive with the minister, the fault is in the ministers and priests themselves, that should instruct and teach them. Wherefore leave the imagine [imagining] of a case well near impossible, and amend your fault of not admonishing and calling the people at your private masses.

Your next proofs are the history of Serapion in Eusebius, *lib.* 6, *ca. ultim.*, who, lying in his death-bed, was served with the sacrament alone; and also the 12th canon of Nicene council, which provideth also for them that were in despair of life, that they lacked not their necessary voyage-provision. Out of these places also you gather sole receiving, and that under one kind. These chances also, that you here in this place recite, be either cases of necessity or great difficulty, as yourself confesseth; and therefore cannot infer any general manner, that either then was, or now should be, used in the common ministration of the sacrament. But neither the history nor yet the canon speaketh generally of all that lie in their death-bed, but only of one sort, that before were restrained from communion, which they called penitents. For the manner of the primitive church was, if a man had either in persecution forsaken the faith, or otherwise grievously offended, that before he could be received to the communion again,

CAP. IX.
Answer to Eusebius and Nicene council.

A.

B.

he had a time of penance appointed him; as three, four, or five years, more or less as the matter required. If it happened, that, before his time of penance were finished, he were at extremity of death, then he should have the sacrament given him, lest he should depart excommunicated, and as one that was not of the church and mystical body of Christ. For this extremity, which then was very common and often, to satisfy men's weak consciences, they were, in the primitive church, driven almost of necessity, both to such kind of sole receiving, and also reserving of the sacrament. Of this sort was that [of] Serapion, that you speak of. Of this sort doth that twelfth canon speak, as it may appear in the other going before. Now, in this necessity and extremity, if they admitted sole receiving, is it a proof that they used it in the common celebration of the sacrament, as you do? By as good reason you may prove, out of the same history, that it were no abuse to have boys and children to minister the sacrament commonly; because, in that extremity, Serapion's boy delivered him the sacrament which the priest sent. Surely in this your manner of defending private mass, wherein you shew yourself to be able to bring nothing for the maintenance thereof, but only extraordinary chances in extremity and necessity, you do much bewray the evil use of it, and manifestly declare, yea, and as it were protest, that in deed it is evil and without all authority or example of the primitive church, if you be not driven to it by necessity and lack of communicants.

You will reply, perhaps, and say, by these examples it may appear, that company in receiving is not of necessity, or if it had been, they would not have used the contrary. Yes, sir, necessity and extremity may cause some kind of God's commandments at times to be omitted; and yet, out of necessity, the same commandments ought necessarily to be observed and kept. The Jews were commanded on the sabbath-day to do no bodily or toiling work. Nevertheless sometimes we read, that, by necessity of their enemies constrained, they kept war and fought on the sabbath-day. Yet can you not say but that commandment was necessary. I said the like before of baptism; and the same must I say in the Lord's supper; that a case of necessity may, perhaps, for a time alter some necessary part of it, and yet not be taken for any general rule. Therefore if ye will receive alone in your mass, or minister under one kind, you must never do it but in extremity; otherwise your proofs help you nothing at all. Yea, but in the history of Serapion but one kind is mentioned, and reservation manifestly appeareth in that it was so ready to be delivered to the messenger. If in their reservation (which they used for cases of extremity) they did keep only the one kind, that is not to be taken for a perpetual rule in the celebration of the sacrament, as I have divers times rehearsed; especially seeing all the doctors, when they spake of the common receiving, signify, as I have before declared, that, according to Christ's institution and doctrine of the apostles, they used both bread and wine.

A.   Albeit I have hitherto so answered you, as I may seem to grant your gathering of ministering under one kind upon this place of Eusebius, I may not omit to advertise you, that you pick more out of that place, than by the words ye are able to justify. For in deed the words seemeth more to make against you than with you. *Parum eucharistiæ (inquit) puero dedit, jussitque ut id infunderet et in os senis instillaret*[1]. "He gave to the boy a small portion of the sacrament of thanksgiving, and bade him steep or soak it, and pour it softly into the old man's mouth." Here note you, that *eucharistia* comprehendeth both bread and wine, by the witness of Justin in his Apology. Where, after he hath shewed, that both bread and the cup, over which thanks were given, was distributed to all present, he addeth: *Hoc alimentum apud nos vocatur eucharistia.* "This nourishment is called the sacrament of thanksgiving." Wherefore the priest in this place gave to the boy a small portion of both parts; and, because the sick and feeble man, who had lien three days speechless, was not able to receive bread dry, he willed the boy so to soak the same in the wine, as he might pour both softly into the old man's mouth, and so he did. That it was this, the words *infudit* and *instillavit* doth declare; which could not be done without liquor. Neither is it likely, that

[1 See note, p. 28, above.]

the priest would will the boy to soak the sacrament consecrated in a liquor not consecrated; and especially if he were of your opinion in transubstantiation. This [Thus] may you see by your own place, that in reservation they used often to keep both kinds; which might well stand with the manner of that time, wherein they did every day communicate; so that the wine also might well tarry until the next day.

The fourteenth canon of Nicene council in no sense doth prove sole receiving, as you would have it seem to do[2]. It appointeth who should minister, and in what order they should receive; first the bishop, then the priests, after the deacons, and so forth other that did communicate. This order taken by that holy council maketh so plainly against the manner of your private mass, as I assure you, I marvel that you could for shame allege it. Who seeth not by this testimony, that all the ministers used commonly to receive together with the bishop being present? Here was not my lord at the high altar, and the residue of his chaplains and priests in sundry chapels celebrating by themselves, but all received together, deacons and all; that it might appear to be a heavenly feast or supper, and not a work or sacrifice to be done of one to the behoof and benefit of a number, that stand by and look on. The council speaketh not here in this point of any extraordinary chance, as it doth in that part that you allege, but of

CAP. X.
Answer to the fourteenth canon of Nicene Council.

[2 See note, pp. 30, 31, above.]

the common ordinary manner which by the authority of the same council was appointed to be used in the church. If we had lacked testimonies for the truth against private mass, we had been much beholden to you, for putting us in mind of this place. I think, such as favour your assertion will smally thank you for bringing in this council. But thanked be God, that you are driven so much to your shifts, as you cannot maintain falsehood, but that you are constrained withal to promote the truth. Where you say, that deacons, in the absence of the bishop and priests, might themselves take forth the sacrament and eat, there appeareth an extraordinary case, as was in Serapion's boy ministering. But yet it saith not, *Ipse proferat et edat*, which would have made gaily with you, but, *Ipsi proferant et edant*. Wherefore here is no cloak at all to cover your private mass or sole receiving, but all expressly against it. For, albeit there be no lay-people here mentioned to receive, yet you understand all the ministers received together. Notwithstanding this place proveth not, but that the people at the same time used to receive with the ministers. For the bishop, priests, deacons, with the residue of the clergy and the people also, communicated all together at one time. But for order's sake the priests and clergy stood together, and the lay-people also by themselves, and received after the clergy. Therefore shall you sometime read, that certain of the clergy, for punishment, as it were degraded, were *rejecti in laicam com-*

munionem[1], that is, enjoined to stand with the lay-people at the communion.

In handling of this place, whereas indeed all the arguments that you have brought are nothing but writhings of extraordinary cases, yet, as though you had great store of strong and invincible proofs, and such as no man can stand against, you would seem to yield unto us of your own right; and, upon a confidence of your cause, as it were to give us an argument, that you could wring out of this canon, for receiving under one kind. Indeed, such be the residue of your wrestings, and therefore you might have placed this among them as one of the chief. By the like argument, yea, and better too, you may prove out of the same place, that priests also received but only the body and not the blood; because it saith, *Corpus Christi porrigant*, and mentioneth not *sanguinem*. The like you shall read in many places of the old Fathers, where one part only is mentioned, when they speak of the priests

A.

[[1] Thus the Trullan Council speaks of offenders being ἐν τῷ τῶν λαϊκῶν ἀπωθούμενοι τόπῳ. Can. 21. Conc. ed. Hardouin, Tom. III. col. 1669. And Pope Cornelius in a letter to Fabius, bishop of Antioch, says of a schismatical bishop returning to the Church,—ᾧ καὶ ἐκοινωνήσαμεν ὡς λαϊκῷ. EUSEB. Hist. Eccl. Lib. VI. c. 43, in Ep. Rom. Pontif. ed. Coustant. Paris. 1721. col. 149. And Cyprian directs, that schismatical priests and deacons "hac conditione suscipi cum revertuntur, ut communicent laici."—Ep. ad Steph. Pap. de Concil. Op. ed. cit. Ep. 72, p. 197. And Pope Gelasius directs Rufinus (according to Gratian) respecting an offending clergyman,—in aliquo eum monasterio retrudas, laica tantummodo sibi communione concessa.—GRATIAN. Decret. P. I. dist. 55. cap. 13. Corp. Jur. Canon. ed. cit. Tom. I. col. 191.]

receiving; and yet both are understood. If you will upon this gather, that deacons used but one kind, I will infer upon the same place, that priests also used the like manner. But a reasonable man will easily conceive, that in speaking of one part both is understood. For in the Acts of the Apostles the whole celebration of the sacrament is termed, "breaking of bread;" whereby we must not gather, that apostles used only bread in ministration of the Lord's supper. I marvel why you make such courtesy to recite this for a proof of one kind then used, seeing the best of your collections for this matter be even of the same sort. Is not your conjecture out of Tertullian, Cyprian, Ambrose, even in the same manner gathered; for that they seem to mention but the one part only? And yet you make such a brag upon them, as you count all such to lack discretion, as will not by-and-by, without contradiction, yield unto them and acknowledge them invincible. Indeed, it standeth you upon, seeing your proofs are of themselves so slender, somewhat to help them with stout words; that men may be almost afraid to doubt of them.

[Acts ii. 46.]

B. You object to us, that we dally, when we press you with the words of Christ's institution, *Accipite, manducate, bibite, dividite;* and yet you will urge the words of the Fathers, as though every syllable in them were in like manner to be scanned as the words of the Bible, written wholly by the inspiration of the Holy Ghost. But indeed you declare of what authority you count Christ's words, that esteem it a dallying to repeat often his commandments. Did Cyprian, think you, dally, when, in one Epistle to Cæcilius, he doth well near twenty times repeat and beat upon this,—that the sacrament is to be ministered in no other manner than Christ himself did use it? Did he dally, when he pressed upon the matter in this wise?—" If in that sacrifice, that is Christ himself, none but Christ is to be followed, then must we obey and do that Christ did, and willed to be done; when as he in his gospel saith,—If you do that I bid you, then I call you not servants but friends. And that Christ is only to be heard, his Father witnesseth from heaven, saying,—This is my dear beloved Son; him you must hear. Wherefore, if only Christ is to be heard, we must not give ear what other did before, but what Christ did before all. Neither must we follow men's custom, but God's truth; seeing he saith by his prophet,—In vain they worship me, teaching men's traditions and doctrines. And again, the Lord saith, in the gospel,—You reject my commandment for your own tradition. And in another place, —He that breaketh one of these least commandments and so teacheth, shall be called least in the kingdom of God. If then it be not lawful to alter one of the least commandments, how much less may we alter so great and weighty commandments as these are, so nigh touching the Sacrament of the Lord's Passion and our redemption; or to turn them to any other purpose, by man's tradition, than the Lord ordained them[1]."

These are not my sayings, but word by word as they lie in that holy father; and will you say, that he cavilleth or dallieth, when he thus urgeth Christ's institution to be kept, and would have nothing therein to be altered for any cause that man could devise? The matter that he wrote against, was of no more effect than these are of sole receiving and ministering one part of the Sacrament; and yet is he so earnest, as you see, with a great number of words more to the same purpose. Think you not, they could have brought for the use of water

[[1] Nam si in sacrificio quod Christus obtulerit non nisi Christus sequendus est; utique id nos obaudire et facere oportet, quod Christus fecit, et quod faciendum esse mandavit; quando ipse in Evangelio dicat: Si feceritis quod mando vobis, jam non dico vos servos, sed amicos. Et quod Christus debeat solus audiri, Pater etiam de cœlo contestatur, dicens: Hic est Filius meus dilectissimus in quo bene sensi; ipsum audite. Quare si solus Christus audiendus est, non debemus attendere, quid alius ante nos faciendum putaverit, sed quid qui ante omnes est Christus prior fecerit. Neque enim hominis consuetudinem sequi oportet, sed Dei veritatem; cum per Isaiam prophetam Deus loquatur et dicat: Sine causa autem colunt me, mandata et doctrinas hominum docentes; et iterum Dominus in Evangelio hoc idem repetat, dicens: Rejicitis mandatum Dei, ut traditionem vestram statuatis. Sed et alio in loco ponit et dicit: Qui solverit unum ex mandatis istis minimis, et sic docuerit homines, minimus vocabitur in regno cœlorum. Quod si nec minima de mandatis Dominicis licet solvere, quanto magis tam magna, tam grandia, tam ad ipsum Dominicæ passionis et nostræ redemtionis sacramentum pertinentia, fas non est infringere; aut in aliud, quam quod divinitus institutum sit, humana traditione mutare!—CYPRIAN. Epist. ad Cæcil. Op. ed. cit. Part. II. Epist. 63, pp. 154, 155.]

only the examples of holy men, and also goodly considerations in appearance? Yes, certainly that, and it is to be gathered in Cyprian, that such were alleged. But he crieth still, we must follow Christ, and do as he did, and no otherwise. The truth is therefore of this your cavilling, that Christ's words and institution is so flat against you, as you have no other shift to escape, but either, so to imminish and debase the weight of Christ's commandments, as they may appear but indifferent counsels; or, so to amplify and extol the Church's power, that the same, upon gaily devised considerations, may alter and take away those things that he hath appointed to be used. Remember how earnest you have been in magnifying your own traditions; as, that the sacrament can be consecrated after no other fashion than you have set forth in your mass; in that the leaving away of one vestment, alb, tunicle, stole, the omitting of one kneeling, crossing, or other like gesture, is counted a heinous matter. And shall it then be esteemed a cavilling or dallying, precisely to require the same to be used according to the manner by Christ the author taught and set forth in the holy Evangelists? This is it that Christ said to the Pharisees, that they magnified their own traditions, and left undone God's commandments. Repeat you as oft as you list against us, that we cavil when we urge Christ's institution; and you shall hear as oft at our hand, that you worship God in vain with your traditions, when you depart from his holy word.

CAP. XI.
Answer to Cyprian, *De lapsis*.

As touching the history that you recite out of Cyprian, *De lapsis*, you make me doubt of divers things which I should think most true; either, that you had not seen the place yourself, but as you found it piecemeal recited of some other, so to have used it; or else, that you thought us so unskilful and negligent, as we neither knew the place, nor would seek to examine it; or lastly, that of purpose you did abuse the simplicity and ignorance of them that you conveyed your writing unto; which commonly believe all that you say without examination; and therefore do you allege for yourself that maketh expressly against you, if the place be read, which in Cyprian is in this wise: "The child being among the holy company, was not able to abide our suffrages and prayers; but the ignorant soul, in the simple and young years, sometime with weeping and crying did startle; sometime with trouble and anguish of mind tossed hither and thither; and as it were by a tormentor constraining it, by such means as it could, did confess the guilt of the fact, (meaning the eating of the idol offering,) and, when the residue of the celebration was ended, the deacon began to offer the cup to them that were present; and after other had received, and the child's course was come, the babe, as it were by institution of God, turned away the face, held the mouth and lips together, and refused the cup. Yet the deacon continued, and, although the infant strived against it, poured some of the sacrament of the Lord's blood into her mouth. Then followed yexing and vomiting[1]." Here were gathered together with Cyprian, not priests only, but laymen, women, and children also; and you see the cup of our Lord's blood was offered to all, and all drank in order without exception. Neither is here anything that by conjecture can lead a man to think otherwise, but that this was the common manner then used. How then can you gather by the extraordinary chance, which you recited before out of the same Tertullian and Cyprian, that the laity then used to receive the one kind of bread only; whereas this place, brought by yourself, sheweth, that in celebration they used the cup also? The child, you say, in this history, received but wine only, and so one kind. That you make probable, because the child, that had received the idol-offering, was not vexed, before the deacon gave her the wine. But this reason is plain against Cyprian's words, who saith, the child was wonderfully vexed so soon as they began to pray. Therefore, by this place, you can no more gather, that the child received only wine, than Cyprian himself and the residue of the company. But if it were so, is it not most evident, that it was, either because the child was so young that it could not, or so troubled that it would not, take the sacrament of the body; and so at that time did of necessity, which otherwise he would not have done? Why, ye will say, my purpose was to prove no more but that in

[1 See note, p. 34, above.]

necessity one kind might be used. Although I should grant you that, yet it followeth not, but, at other times, of necessity both parts of the sacrament should be taken. For I have divers times said, that necessity hath no law, and may cause a commandment of God to be omitted, which, out of that extremity, ought of necessity to be kept under pain of God's displeasure. By this history it is plain, how necessary that time did think it, that all present should communicate with the ministers: seeing the deacon would not suffer so much as the little infant to go without some part, although she strived against him, and scantly could force her to take it. This maketh against the fashion of your Private Mass; where, not infants and children, but other ministers and the residue of all the congregation stand looking on, and no man receiveth, nor is provided for, but only one priest, that consecrateth and receiveth all himself. Your handling of this place of Cyprian may be a sufficient proof to all men, how soundly and truly you interpret other men's writings, and how sincerely you judge of them, that is, by violence as it were to strain them to say that which they never meant.

In like manner you do a little after in Luther and Melancthon, saying that they count it a thing indifferent to communicate the lay people under one kind, and that a general council may take order in it as a thing of no necessity. Sir, it had been plain and sound dealing, that you should have recited some place where they had so said; but that ye were not able to do. For any man that hath been conversant in their works, may right well judge that it is not so. I will not trouble you with looking on many places. There is a little treatise of Melancthon's entitled *De usu integri sacramenti;* in which ye shall find divers arguments concluding the necessity of both kinds, and that they sin and grievously offend, that do restrain the people from one part of the sacrament. But I perceive this is your common fashion, to make doctors and writers to speak whatsoever you would have them to speak.

Now sir, if ye have no better proofs and testimonies out of the holy Scriptures and old Fathers, than these which ye have in this your Apology alleged, I assure you, the challenge that before was made may justly be again repeated: and it may be said to you, that you have out of the Scripture nor syllable nor tittle, out of the ancient doctors nor sentence nor half sentence, that doth directly prove either your private mass or communion under one kind to the laity. For all that here you have uttered be nothing but writhed conjectures upon cases extraordinary, and shifts of extremity, to prove a continual or general rule to be observed in the church of Christ, contrary to the example and order by himself appointed. Wherefore there is no cause, that you should so confidently conclude, as though you had profoundly proved the matter, and given us,

CAP. XII.

A.

as you say, an occasion to discuss and more curiously to examine the residue of our doctrines. Think you not, but the meanest of a great number in this realm (although they seem but babes and children to you) have known a great deal more than you have here alleged; and could have spoken better for you, than you have yet for yourself. And yet, when they had all said, it had been nothing in comparison of the very truth. It is but a jollity in you, that ye do so roll up the names of doctors, saying, Tertullian is against you, Cyprian is against you, Eusebius is against you, &c. As though you had alleged out of every one of them a number of testimonies for the declaration of their minds; whereas you have brought out of them all but a few bye sentences, of which the more part make nothing against us, and some expressly with us. These be the titles of the empty boxes that you do use to brag upon. But as you will say, your boxes are not altogether empty; so will I answer, they have but little good stuff in them, and some of them contain medicines contrary to the diseases that they are applied unto: which is the part neither of good physician nor true apothecary. A good physician, when the body is troubled with divers diseases, will so endeavour to cure and heal the one, that he do not exasperate and hurt the other. But you, by Chrysostom, Cyprian, and Nicene council, in such sort help reservation, as, by the same, you clean mar your private masses, and ministering under one kind to the laity.

Neither will I ever think, that the best and greatest learned of your clergy can bring much better stuff out of their store of the doctors, than you have done. Wherefore their bonds of recognisance and possession of the truth (as you say) hath been fair clokes for them to hold their peace, whereas indeed they have in these points or little or nothing to say for themselves. And surely, if I had been of your sort, I would have wished, that you also had been bound in recognisance, if that would have stayed you from writing: for both your reasons and authorities by you uttered, though they seem to yourself never so strong, doth rather bewray your part, than pithily defend it. But if you and yours had never so great store of armour, provision, and furniture, as, to the terror of men, you would pretend to have; yet ye should never be able to bear down the manifest truth, so evidently appearing in the words of Christ's institution, nor the witnesses of the primitive Church agreeing with the same.

Therefore the thundering in of the authority of the holy catholic Church, the prescription of 1500 years, the consent of most parts of Christendom, the holiness and learning of so many godly Fathers as hath been these 900 years, the age and slender learning of those that stand against you, doth nothing at all either fear us, or move us to suspect that doctrine, which, by Christ's authority and witness of the apostles, we know to be true. We have been accustomed of long time to those vain voices. *Answer to the argument of multitude, continuance of time, &c.*

We see they all be either manifestly false, or at the least of small effect. These are the mists which you have alway cast before the eyes of the simple and ignorant, as it were to blind and amaze them; to the end that, either they may not see the truth, when it is brought to them, or, if they see it, to make them suspect it, when they hear, that 1500 years the more part of the world have been of contrary opinion. But this is evidently false that you say. For 600 years after Christ and more, these doctrines were never heard of in the Church, much less received and allowed. Yea, and in the time following, neither did they so soon take place, as you would have them seem to do; and when they were rooted, God stirred up from time to time divers in all ages that reproved them. Therefore you cannot justly brag of quiet possession so long time. But by your spiritual powers, that occupied the place of the Church, such men were disgraced, and their doctrine and books abolished, and, so much as might be, brought out of memory: and on the contrary part, by pernicious flatterers, the works of ancient Fathers corrupted, [and] other new works and epistles forged in their name; that by this means your doctrine, which is but new indeed in comparison of truth, might have a face or vizard of antiquity, thereby the sooner to creep into men's consciences. Shall we think, that your Donation of Constantine, and a number of Epistles, attributed to the ancient bishops of Rome, be their true monuments? Doth not the barbarousness of the style, the repugnancy to the histories and writers of that time, the unfit wresting of places of holy Scripture, so evidently appear in them, as a child almost may perceive them to be forged, and not to agree with the spirit of the primitive Church? Be not yourselves ashamed of the counterfeit Donation of Constantine, wherewith the see of Rome a long time blinded the princes of the earth, and made them almost slaves unto it? Be not there a number of places in your decrees fathered upon the old doctors, which either be not in them at all, or else otherwise than they be there recited? And shall we think, then, that truth hath been so long on your part, when forging and falsehood hath most maintained your doctrine? Add to this, that Greece and all the East churches never received private mass, communion under one kind, prohibition of marriage in priests, purgatory, the supremacy of Rome, nor a number more of your errors; yea, and at this day think and do contrary to you in those things. And will you then so falsely bear men in hand, that the whole Church was always of your opinion?

But be it so, that the most part of Christendom 900 years hath taught as you do. Is that a sufficient argument to reject a doctrine evident by the word of God? May not all Christianity be clean defaced, if such arguments of continuance of time and multitude of persons should be rules to govern men's consciences? Might not the Gentiles have alleged the like against the apostles and their successors? Might not they have

said, and said more truly than you, that
the worshipping of their gods had continued,
not hundreds, but thousands of years? that
the whole world held with them? that the
wise and profound learned philosophers de-
fended their doctrine? that the apostles
were but new heretics, idiots, and unlearned
persons? that their doctrine came from the
doting people of the Jews? that the gods
declared their displeasure and indignations
against the new teaching of Christ, with
seditions, tumults, wars, plagues, dearths,
tempestuous weatherings, and such like?
Might not the Israelites have counted great
folly in the house of Judah, that they would
swerve from them in worshipping of God,
seeing they were ten parts to one? Might
not the priests in the old law, yea, did they
not, allege against the prophets continuance
of time and multitude of doctors, priests,
and Rabbins? Were they not hundreds to
one poor Micheas? Did they not the like
in Christ's time? Did they not beat upon
the long continuance of Moses' law, which,
they said, he came to destroy? Did they
not deface him for his age, his birth, his
manner of life; and for that he taught
otherwise than a number of the godly, wise,
and holy Pharisees? which in those days
had as great opinion of holiness of life, and
deep learning, as the best of your religious
monks or observant friars. Might not the
Turks for continuance and multitude make
a gay face for the confirmation of Mahomet's
law? Might not they say, that it hath
continued 1000 years, yea, and that with

great success and prosperity, as it had been by a singular providence of God? May they not say, and too truly affirm, that they have ten for one Christian? May they not say, that it is not likely, that God would suffer such a number of nations and countries to err so many hundred years? Have they not in many parts of their religion such apparent devotion, as they may shame us christian men? And yet is all most evidently false, and God's truth remaineth stedfast; although it bind itself neither to continuance of time, nor to person, to place, to number, to this colour of life or to that in judgment of the world, but is governed by his divine and inscrutable providence. Wherefore these reasons make no more for you and against us, than they did for the Israelites against the Jews; for the priests against the prophets; for the Jews and Gentiles against Christ and his apostles; for the Turks against us Christians at this day.

Yea but, you will say, the holy catholic Church of Christ teacheth otherwise, which is the witness of truth, and cannot err: especially in those things that appertain unto our faith. For Christ hath promised, that he will never forsake his Church unto the end of the world, but guide it with his Spirit. And his Spirit is not the spirit of error, ignorance, or darkness, but of truth, wisdom, and light. Wherefore none can forsake the guiding and instruction of our holy mother the Church, without manifest peril of their own souls, and such as they *To their objection of the Church's authority.*

do lead from the Church. Indeed this accusation is grievous, and may not lightly be passed of me, although you stay not long upon it. This is that you fear men's consciences withal. This is it that indeed maketh many to stagger in receiving the truth, when they hear you continually beat upon the name of your holy mother the Church, and in words claim that to you, which verily and indeed is not in you. For all be not the sons of Abraham, that brag and avaunt, that they came of Abraham's stock; all be not the people of God, that say, they be the people of God; all be not Israelites, that descended of Israel; all be not christian men in deed, that name themselves Christians. I will therefore in few words declare, what the Church is, and how we may, if we take not good heed, be deceived by the name of the Church, taking the Church of antichrist for the true and right Church of Christ.

First, how necessary indeed it is for a christian man to believe the faith of the holy Church, it may by this appear, that to be born to everlasting life and salvation, to be made the son of God and heir of the kingdom of heaven, of necessity we must be conceived in the womb of the Church of Christ, and, as it were, fostered up in her lap. For she is the mother of all those that are the true children of God; and in her custody Christ hath left the treasure of his grace, by her ministry to be bestowed among his people. Therefore if we covet to have entrance into the kingdom of God, and be partakers of the graces and promises of Christ, I confess we must remain in the faith of his holy Church.

But what is this Church, or how may it be known? Forsooth the Scripture speaketh of the Church of Christ two ways. Sometime as it is indeed before God, and not known alway to man's judgment. Into this Church none be received, but only the children of grace and adoption, and the very members of Christ by sanctifying of the Holy Ghost. This Church doth not comprehend only holy men and saints living on the earth, but all the elect from the beginning of the world. This Church is the pillar of truth, that never continueth in error. This Church is never forsaken of the Spirit of God. This is the holy communion of saints, that in our Creed we profess and acknowledge. But this Church, as after shall appear, doth not always flourish in sight of the world. Sometime the Church is taken for the universal multitude of all those, which, being dispersed through the world, acknowledge one Christ, and, being through baptism admitted into the same, by the use of the Lord's supper openly profess the unity thereof in doctrine and charity. Sometime the Church is taken for the multitude of those that bear rule in the Church. This Church is resembled to a net, which, cast into the sea, bringeth up both good and bad. It is resembled to a field, that hath not only pure corn, but also cockle, darnell, and other weeds. And as we often see, that good corn in some grounds is so choked up and overrun with

What the Church is, and whether it may err.

weeds, as the good grain may hardly be discerned, for that the weeds bear the chief rule; even so in this Church the evil and corrupted doth sometime bear down the better sort, that a man can hardly judge, which be the true members of the Church, which are not. This Church, therefore, for the most number, may be misled, and in many things stray out of the way. This Church may err, and not continually abide in pure and uncorrupt worshipping of God, as I will now with good proof farther declare unto you.

God hath had this his external Church from the beginning of the world, instructed by his holy word, instructed by his Patriarchs and Prophets, instructed by his appointed law and ceremonies; and so continued till the coming of his dear Son Jesus Christ. This Church he called his spouse, his tabernacle, his privy garden, his loved city, his elect and chosen vineyard. But did it alway continue in flourishing estate? Did it alway in like manner retain the truth of God's word that it was taught in the beginning? Did it alway cherish and maintain such ministers as God sent from time to time into it to redress and reform his law according to his holy will? In what state was this Church in Noah's time, when eight only were saved? In what state was it, when the ten tribes forsook the right worshipping of God, and left only the tribe of Judah? In what state was it afterward, when the same one tribe of Judah under divers kings fell to idolatry? In what state was it, when Elias pitifully complained, that he only was left, and all other were departed from God? Where was the external face of the Church at that time? In what state was it, when Esaias, Jeremy, Ezechiel, and all the prophets of God were persecuted and put to death? I pray you, was not Jewry then called the people of God? Had they not at that time the law of God? Did not they use his ceremonies? Did not they brag and make their avaunt, that they could not err? that the truth could not depart from the mouth of their priests and doctors? that they had "the temple of God, the temple of God?" Yes, certainly, they had even then the law of God. They had even then the sacraments and ceremonies by God appointed; or else the prophets would never have used their temple or company of their prayers and ceremonies. Yet how miserably the law of God and his sacraments were corrupted among them, it appeareth by that Esay sayeth: "The silver of the people [Isai. i. 22.] of God is turned into dross." How they entertained the messengers that God sent to reform his law, it is evident in this, that all the prophets were slain among them. This external Church then did err, this external Church refused the truth of God's law; this external Church did persecute the prophets. And yet did not the prophets think, that they could cast them out of his true Church, or make them not true members of his people, to which the promises were made. Neither did the prophets for that cause cease to call for a redress of the pure law and ceremonies of God, and worshipping him according to his holy word. They did not refrain to tell even those that said they were the chosen people of God, the elect vineyard of God, the city and habitation of God, that they had forsaken the law of God, that they followed their own devices, that they worshipped God in vain with their own traditions; and therefore that he would not acknowledge them any more for his people; that he would set his vineyard open to spoil; that he would bring his own city into thraldom and captivity. After the captivity of Babylon, when the same Church was restored, and his people taught by adversity to reform the law, and receive again the right worshipping of God appointed in his word, it continued not many years, but that it was again corrupted horribly, and led far out of the way, following again their own phantasies. For when Christ himself came, for whose cause God had so preserved that people, they said, that they had Moses' law, that they were the seed of Abraham, that they were the chosen people and true Church of God; that he went about to take away the law and destroy the temple, and for that cause did they put him to death. In like manner did they use the apostles: they reproved their doctrine as vain and phantastical; they cast them out of their synagogues as schismatics and heretics. Yea, and when they did this, they had in face of the world those things wherein the Church is counted to consist. They had doctrine out of the law of God. They had the ministry of the same by their priests and doctors. They had the sacrament of circumcision, as the covenant whereby they were admitted as the people of God. They had the other ceremonies, wherein they were practised, to the confirmation of the same. They had the councils whereby they condemned Christ, wherein they condemned the apostles, and refused their doctrine. They blamed their predecessors for that they had killed the prophets; and yet they persecuted Christ and his apostles. Shall we think therefore that the apostles were not of the Church? Or rather shall we judge, that they which have the government of the law and sacraments, and to the world have the face and name of the Church, may so foully err, as they may refuse the true doctrine of God's law, and persecute the ministers and setters forth of the same? There lacked not God's promises among the Jews. There lacked not succession of bishops and priests. There lacked not opinion of great holiness and austerity of life. There lacked not great skill and knowledge of the law of God. And yet is it most evident, that they erred, that they refused the truth, that under the name and gay shew of the Church, in very deed they persecuted the Church.

Why shall we not think that the like may be in this time? Yea, why should we not surely persuade ourselves, by the course of God's doings, and by the testimonies of holy Scripture, that the like is now in this our time? Our Saviour Christ and his apostles have left warning abundantly, that it would be so in his Church, and especially toward the end of the world. Christ himself prophesied, that desolation should stand in the holy place; that is, in the Church. St Paul witnesseth, that Antichrist should sit in the temple of God, that is, in the Church: where it is also signified, not that he should be an abject in the Church, but a power avaunting himself above the name of God. Peter saith, that in the Church should be masters and teachers of lies. Paul affirmeth for surety, that in the latter days such shall come, as shall give ear to doctrine of the devil, forbidding to marry and eat such meats as God had created to be taken with thanksgiving. These things were prophesied to come, not among Turks and Saracens, not among infidels and Pagans, but in the temple of God, in the Church of God, in the society of them that did profess Christ. We have therefore great cause to mark the working of God, by the example of the old Church among the Jews. We see that the prophets were first vexed by those that bare the name of the Church, and should have most gladly received them. We see that in Christ's time and the apostle's, not the Gentiles first refused the comfortable tidings of the gospel, but they that called themselves the people of God, and had among them the custody of his law and ceremonies. Even in like manner we have to think that he will do in this time, seeing he hath of the same forewarned us. For even as the old law and religion of the Jews was a

[Matt. xxiv. 15.]
[2 Thess. ii. 4.]
[2 Pet. ii. 1.]
[1 Tim. iv. 1—4.]

shadow and pattern of the true religion brought in by Christ; so the state and manner of that Church may well resemble the state of Christ's Church in the latter time. As the old Church, therefore, toward the end did forsake the law and right use of God's ceremonies, and, being divided in sundry sects, devised new worshippings according to their own phantasies; insomuch that, for the maintenance thereof, they refused Christ and his apostles: so, in like manner, may we justly think, that the Church after Christ, toward the end of the world, shall depart from the truth of God's word and right ministration of his sacraments, cleaving to their own interpretations; and being divided in sundry sects of religion, for the defence of the same, shall refuse and cast out of the Church such as God will send to renew the truth of his holy word and gospel. Wherefore it ought to comfort and confirm us, and cause us to think, that we be indeed in the Church, rather than to fear us; seeing they, that in the pomp and glorious face of the world seem to have the government of the Church, doth refuse us, and take us to be none of the Church. For such they were always, that from the beginning refused and oppressed the truth; such they were that vexed the prophets; such they were that refused Christ; such they were that persecuted his apostles.

Here perhaps some curious conscience will be pricked, and think it is not likely, that God of his great mercy would suffer his Church and so great a number of people to err so many hundred years. But we must beware, how by our reason of likelihood we enter into God's judgment and unscrutable providence. We must think of him as the course of his doings sheweth us. We must think of him as his holy word teacheth us. We must not think of him as our fond reason will lead us. Is it not marvellous, think you, and to our judgment unscrutable, that thousands of years he suffered all the nations of the earth to be nursled in idolatry, and opened his knowledge to only one little people of the Jews? Is it not marvellous, that, of twelve parts of that one people, he suffered ten and a half to forsake him at one time; yea, and that one part that remained, not a few times clean to give over the true worshipping of God; so that in those days he might scant seem to have any true Church upon the whole face of the earth? Be not these things beyond the likelihoods of man's feeble reason? May we not say with St Paul, "O unscrutable and bottomless deepness of his divine judgment," and leave to seek what is likely in his doings? The Jews were his chosen people, from which the Saviour of the world should rise. They had among them his law and ceremonies, his abundant promises and sacraments. They had his tabernacle, out of the which he, as present, spake unto them. If then the deepness of God's judgment were such toward them, that he suffered them so oft and so long to go astray; and since Christ's time most miserably 1560 years hath scattered them upon the earth; may we not fear the

[Rom. xi. 33.]

like also among us in this latter time? Doth not St Paul put us in fear, that, if God did break away the natural branches of the olive, he would also, if cause were given, cut off those that were but graffed on beside nature? Doth not Christ in the gospel forewarn us, that in the latter days should be such mischief and blindness in the Church, that even the elect should be in danger to be seduced? And shall we then hope at that time to see the true Church in so triumphant glory of the world, as it shall make even the greatest emperors and princes of the earth in world[1], might, and power, subject unto it? Truly that agreeth not with Christ's prophecy, nor the warnings of the apostles, wherein they tell us of the great danger that shall happen in the Church toward the end of the world[2].

[Rom. xi. 21.]

[Matt. xxiv. 24; Mark xiii. 22.]

That it may not be thought to be my only phantasy, that the adversary of Christ shall in the latter days sit in the Church, and bear the face of religion, hear you what Hilary saith, *Contra Auxentium;* in whose time the Arians, by the furtherance of the emperor and a number of bishops, took on them the name of the Catholics, and persecuted the true christian Church. "Ye do ill," saith he, "to be in love with walls; ye do ill to worship the Church of God in gay houses and buildings; ye do ill to bring the name of peace under them. Is it not certain,

[1 The word *world* here is probably a misprint for *wealth.*]
[2 As for instance, 2 Thess. ii. 3 et seq.; 2 Tim. ii. 1 et seq.; 2 Pet. iii. 3 et seq.]

that Antichrist shall sit in them? Mountains, woods, marishes, prisons, dens, are more safe for me. For in those the prophets, either voluntarily abiding, or cast thither by violence, did prophesy by the Spirit of God[1]." How could a man more plainly declare, that the true Church both then was, and after should be, vexed and persecuted by those that, in sight and power of external government, were taken for the Church? It is notable also that Augustine hath, *De Civit. Dei*, lib. 20, speaking of Antichrist,—*Rectius putant etiam Latine dici sicut in Græco est; non in templo, sed in templum Dei sedeat, tanquam ipse sit templum Dei, quod est Ecclesia:* "Some think it were better spoken in Latin as it is in the Greek, as to say, that Antichrist should sit, not in the temple of God, but as the temple of God; as though himself were the temple of God, which is the Church[2]." What Bernard did think of the Church in his time, above 400 years ago, it appeareth

[1 Unum moneo, cavete Antichristum : male enim vos parietum amor cepit, male Ecclesiam Dei in tectis ædificiisque veneramini, male sub his pacis nomen ingeritis. Anne ambiguum est, in his Antichristum esse sessurum? Montes mihi, et silvæ, et lacus, et carceres, et voragines sunt tutiores: in his enim prophetæ, aut manentes aut demersi, Dei Spiritu prophetabant.—HILAR. Lib. contra Auxent. § 12. Op. ed. Bened. Paris. 1693, col. 1269.]

[2 Unde nonnulli, non ipsum principem, sed universum quodammodo corpus ejus, id est, ad eum pertinentem hominum multitudinem simul cum ipso suo principe hoc loco intelligi Antichristum volunt: rectiusque putant etiam Latine dici, sicut in Græco est, non *in templo Dei,* sed *in templum Dei sedeat,* tamquam ipse sit templum Dei, quod est Ecclesia.— AUGUST. De Civit. Dei. Lib. xx. cap. 19. § 2. Op. ed. Bened. Paris. Tom. VII. col. 597.]

in divers places. "There is no sound part now," saith he, "in the clergy; it remaineth therefore that the man of sin be revealed." And in another place: "All my friends be now become my foes, all my maintainers are now become adversaries. The servants of Christ do service to Antichrist³." If I should recite out of authors and histories all such testimonies as serveth to this purpose, I should be a great deal longer than this place requireth. I will therefore at this time omit them.

[³ These two citations, which seem to be quoted *memoriter*, as no reference even is given to the works in which they are found, are clearly derived from the two following passages:

Ipsa quoque ecclesiasticæ dignitatis officia in turpem quæstum et tenebrarum negotium transiere: nec in his salus animarum, sed luxus quæritur divitiarum. Propter hoc tondentur, propter hoc frequentant ecclesias, missas celebrant, psalmos decantant. Pro episcopatibus et archidiaconatibus impudenter hodie decertatur, ut ecclesiarum reditus in superfluitatis et vanitatis usus dissipentur. Superest jam ut reveletur homo peccati, filius perditionis.—BERNARD. in Psalm. *Qui habitat.* Serm. VI. § 7. Op. ed. Mabillon. Paris. 1690. Vol. I. col. 838.

Serpit hodie putida tabes per omne corpus Ecclesiæ, et quo latius, eo desperatius; eoque periculosius, quo interius. Nam si insurgeret apertus inimicus hæreticus, mitteretur foras et aresceret: si violentus inimicus, absconderet se forsitan ab eo. Nunc vero quem ejiciet, aut a quo abscondet se? Omnes amici, et omnes inimici: omnes necessarii, et omnes adversarii: omnes domestici, et nulli pacifici: omnes proximi, et omnes quæ sua sunt quærunt. Ministri Christi sunt, et serviunt Antichristo.— EJUSD. Comm. in Cantica, Serm. XXXIII. § 15. Ibid. Vol. I. col. 1392, 1393.

Similar remarks occur, as our author observes, in divers other places of his works; as, for instance, in the Preface to his Liber de vita S. Malachiæ; Op. Vol. I. col. 657, 658.]

Seeing therefore it doth evidently appear, that, in the latter time, they shall bear the name of the Church, which indeed be not the right Church, we must look diligently, that we give not over to every power that will claim the name of the Church, but consider whether the true mark of the holy Church be among them. Christ, the true pastor, noting which were his sheep, saith: "My sheep will hear my voice." And as by his word and voice he calleth them into his fold, so by his sacraments there he marketh them. The right Church therefore, as the fold of Christ, hath the true word of God and use of his sacraments according to the same, for the due marks thereof. So much then as the word of God and use of the sacraments be corrupted among any people or congregation, so far shall that company be from the state of the true and perfect Church of Christ. Therefore it is easy to judge, what is to be thought of them that leave the word of God, and worship him well near altogether with their own devised phantasies.

That the Scripture, which is the voice and word of God, is the true trial of the Church, we have good authority in the ancient Fathers. St Augustine, *Contra Petilianum*, cap. 2. "The controversy is between us and the Donatists," saith he, "where the Church is. Therefore what shall we do? Shall we seek it in our own words, or in the words of our Lord Jesus Christ, the head thereof? I think we ought rather to seek it in his words, that is truth, and best knoweth his body[1]." Therefore they be not to be counted the Church, that with their own words will say they be the Church; but they whose doctrine agreeth with the word of Christ that is head of the Church. In like manner hath Chrysostom, *in Mat.* cap. 14: "Wherefore," saith he, "in this time all christian men ought to resort to the Scriptures; because in this time, since heresy is come into the churches, there can be no other proof of true Christianity, nor any other refuge for christian men, desiring to know the true faith, but only the holy Scriptures. For, before it was shewed by many means, which was the Church of Christ, which was Gentility. But now, to them that will know, which is the right Church of Christ, there is no means but only by the Scriptures[2]."

[1] Inter nos autem et Donatistas quæstio est, ubi sit hoc corpus, id est, ubi sit Ecclesia. Quid ergo facturi sumus? In verbis nostris eam quæsituri, an in verbis capitis sui, Domini nostri Jesu Christi? Puto quod in illius potius verbis eam quærere debemus, qui veritas est, et optime novit corpus suum. *Novit* enim *Dominus qui sunt ejus.*—AUGUST. ad Cathol. Epist. contr. Donatist., *vulgo*, De Unit. Eccles. Lib. unus. [in prior. quibusdam edd., Contra Petil. Epist. Lib. unus] cap. 2. Op. ed. Bened. Paris. Tom. IX. col. 338.]

[2] Et quare jubet in hoc tempore omnes Christianos conferre se ad Scripturas? Quia in tempore hoc, ex quo obtinuit hæresis illas ecclesias, nulla probatio potest esse veræ Christianitatis, neque refugium potest esse Christianorum aliud, volentium cognoscere fidei veritatem, nisi Scripturæ divinæ. Antea enim multis modis ostendebatur, quæ esset Ecclesia Christi, et quæ Gentilitas; nunc autem nullo modo cognoscitur volentibus cognoscere quæ sit vera Ecclesia Christi nisi tantummodo per Scripturas.— CHRYSOST. Opus Imperf. in Matth. Hom. 49. Op. ed. Bened. Paris. Tom. VI. App. p. 204.]

St Augustine hath the like in many words in the 16 cap. *Contra Epistolam Petiliani,* which I let pass here for brevity's sake. The place beginneth in this wise: *Utrum Donatistæ Ecclesiam teneant, non nisi divinarum Scripturarum canonicis libris ostendant. Quia nec nos propterea dicimus nobis credere oportere, quod in Ecclesia Christi sumus, &c.*[1] Wherefore a christian conscience, that in this dangerous time will walk safely, must take the word of God to be his only stay; must take the holy Scripture to be as well the rule whereby he shall

[[1] Sed utrum ipsi Ecclesiam teneant, non nisi de divinarum Scripturarum canonicis libris ostendant; quia nec nos propterea dicimus nobis credi oportere, quod in Ecclesia Christi sumus, quia ipsam, quam tenemus, commendavit Milevitanus Optatus, vel Mediolanensis Ambrosius, vel alii innumerabiles nostræ communionis episcopi; aut quia nostrorum collegarum conciliis ipsa prædicata est; aut quia per totum orbem in locis sanctis, quæ frequentat nostra communio, tanta mirabilia vel exauditionum vel sanitatum fiunt... Quæcunque talia in Catholica fiunt, ideo sunt approbanda, quia in Catholica fiunt; *non ideo ipsa manifestatur Catholica, quia hæc in ea fiunt.* Ipse Dominus Jesus cum resurrexisset a mortuis, et discipulorum oculis videndum manibusque tangendum corpus suum offerret, ne quid tamen fallaciæ se pati arbitrarentur, magis eos testimoniis Legis et Prophetarum et Psalmorum confirmandos esse judicavit, ostendens ea de se impleta, quæ fuerant tanto ante prædicta. Sic et Ecclesiam suam commendavit, dicens, "prædicari in nomine suo pœnitentiam et remissionem peccatorum per omnes gentes, incipientibus ab Ierusalem." Hoc in Lege et Prophetis et Psalmis esse scriptum ipse testatus est: hoc ejus ore commendatum tenemus. *Hæc sunt causæ nostræ documenta, hæc fundamenta, hæc firmamenta.*—Aug. ad Catholicos Ep. contra Donatist., *vulgo,* De Unit. Eccles. Lib. unus. (in prior. quibusdam edd., Contra Petil. Epist. Lib. unus) § 50. Op. ed. Bened. Paris. Tom. IX. col. 373.]

measure the true pattern of the Church, as the very touchstone whereby he must try all the doctrine of the same. "For God in time past spake by his prophets many and sundry ways, but last of all by his dear Son:" whose doctrine how perfect it was, the woman of Samaria witnesseth, saying,—"When Messias cometh, he shall tell us all things." And the same Messias himself saith,—"I have made known to you all that I have heard of my Father." And therefore, sending his apostles, he saith,— "Teach them to observe all that I have commanded." As if he had said, ye shall declare unto the Gentiles, not whatsoever shall seem good to yourselves, but those things that I have commanded you. Those things therefore are to be heard; those things we must stay upon; in those we must seek our salvation and life. Whatsoever is not agreeing with them must be cast off, and counted of no force. So saith Origen: "We must needs call the holy Scriptures to witness: for our senses and declarations without those witnesses have no credit[2]." So saith Hierome: "What hath not authority in the Scriptures, is even as lightly contemned as it is spoken[3]." And again, *in Psal.* lxxxvi.: "Consider what he saith;

[Heb. i. 1, 2.]

[John iv. 25.]

[John xv. 15.]

[Matt. xxviii. 20.]

In Hierem. Hom. I.

[[2] Μάρτυρας δεῖ λαβεῖν τὰς γραφάς· ἀμάρτυροι γὰρ αἱ ἐπιβολαὶ ἡμῶν καὶ αἱ ἐξηγήσεις ἄπιστοί εἰσιν.—ORIG. In Jerem. Hom. 1. § 7. Op. ed. Delarue, Paris. 1740. Tom. III. p. 129.]

[[3] Hoc quia de Scripturis non habet auctoritatem, eadem facilitate contemnitur qua probatur.—HIERON. Comment. in Matth. c. 23, vv. 35, 36. Op. ed. Vallars. Venet. 1766 et seq. Tom. VII. col. 190.]

'Which were in it,' not which be in it. So that, except the apostles, whatsoever should be spoken afterward, let it be cut off; let it not have authority. Therefore be one never so holy, after the apostles, be he never so eloquent, he hath not authority; because the Lord will make his declaration in the writing of people and princes that were in it[1]." In that place Hierome at large declareth, that the doctrine of God must be proved by such writings as were in the Church until the apostles' time, and those that after followed to be of no sufficient authority, were they never so holy. Let us stay therefore upon the canonical Scriptures and holy word of God. "For," saith St Cyprian, "hereof arise schisms, because we seek not to the head, nor have recourse to the spring, nor keep the commandments of the heavenly master[2]." "Let us ask Peter," saith Ambrose, "let us ask Paul, if we will find out the truth[3]." And Christ

[1] Videte quid dicat: *Qui fuerunt*, non, qui sunt: ut, exceptis Apostolis, quodcunque aliud postea dicetur, abscindatur, non habeat postea auctoritatem. Quamvis ergo sanctus sit aliquis post apostolos, quamvis disertus sit, non habet auctoritatem; quoniam Dominus narrat in Scriptura populorum et principum horum qui fuerunt in ea.—HIERON. Brev. in Psalm. Ps. 86 (apud nos 87) v. 6. Op. ed. ead. Tom. VII. Append.]

[2] Hæreses invenit [i. e. "Inimicus"] et schismata, quibus subverteret fidem, veritatem corrumperet, scinderet unitatem...Rapit de ipsa Ecclesia homines...Hoc eo fit, fratres dilectissimi, dum ad veritatis originem non reditur, nec caput quæritur, nec magistri cœlestis doctrina servatur.—CYPRIAN. De Unit. Eccles. Op. ed. cit. P. I. p. 105.]

[3 The passage that comes nearest to this in the works of Ambrose (as far as I am aware), and cer-

himself biddeth us "search the Scriptures," [John v. 39.] and not presume of our own spirit upon unwritten verities beside the word of God. What credit is to be given to those that so speak, Chrysostom teacheth us: "As Christ," saith he, "when he understood, that they said commonly of him, that he was a deceiver, to purge himself of that suspicion, witnessed that he spake not of himself, because he spake out of the law and prophets; even so if any man, saying that he hath the Holy Ghost, speaketh of himself, and not out of the gospels, we must not believe him; for as Christ said, the Holy Ghost shall not speak of himself, but shall declare unto you those things that it hath heard; that is, those things that I have spoken, he shall confirm[4]." These

tainly expresses its sense, is the following:—Sed nolo argumento credas, sancte Imperator, et nostræ disputationi : Scripturas interrogemus, interrogemus apostolos, interrogemus prophetas, interrogemus Christum.—AMBROS. De Fide, Lib. I. c. 6. Op. ed. Bened. Paris. Tom. II. col. 451.]

[4 This citation is a sort of condensed paraphrase of a passage in a homily on the Holy Spirit, attributed to Chrysostom, but now generally considered not from his pen. It is reckoned as his by Photius. Sir H. Savile says, "Vel Chrysostomi, vel, quod potius reor, alterius alicujus ex illa erudita antiquitate." The Benedictines adjudge it to be spurious, though able, and of an age not much later than Chrysostom's. The following are the words which our author seems to have had more especially in his eye :—'Επεὶ οὖν οἱ ψευδοπροφῆται ἀφ' ἑαυτῶν ἐκήρυττον, ὁ σωτὴρ ἀποδυόμενος τὴν ὑπόνοιαν λέγει· ἐγὼ ἀπ' ἐμαυτοῦ οὐ λαλῶ...'Επεὶ οὖν πλάνος ἐνομίζετο, λέγει, ἐγὼ ἀπ' ἐμαυτοῦ οὐ λαλῶ, ἀλλ' ἀπὸ νόμου, ἀπὸ προφητῶν, ὅσα ἤκουσα παρὰ τοῦ Πατρός. ...'Εάν τις οὖν τῶν ὀνομαζόντων ἔχειν Πνεῦμα, λέγῃ τι ἀφ' ἑαυτοῦ, καὶ μὴ ἀπὸ τῶν εὐαγγελίων, μὴ

words of Chrysostom clean overthroweth the ground of all your unwritten verities beside the word of God, much more such doctrines as be expressly against the same, as is your sole receiving and communion under one kind. Wherefore neither your multitude of sundry nations, and great learned clerks, neither the continuance of 900 years, (if it were so), neither the name of your holy mother the Church, which you so often repeat, can be any sure proof of your doctrines, without the express testimonies of the Scripture to witness the same. For the Holy Ghost, which you assure your Church of, doth not speak of himself (saith Chrysostom), but confirmeth that Christ spake before.

After that you have at your pleasure in sundry parts of your treatise charged him that you write against with folly, rashness, arrogancy, and impudency, even in those points that the same crimes may be more justly returned to yourself and yours; in this place also you endeavour to debase and imminish his estimation, extenuating his age, continuance in study of holy Scripture, and manner of life, in comparison of your late holy fathers, which you do greatly extol. Such is your shifts, when the matter will not help itself, to transfer your talk to

[*i. e.* Bp. Jewel.]

πιστεύσητε......'Εκ τοῦ μὴ λέγειν τὰ γεγραμμένα, ἀλλὰ τὰ ἀφ' ἑαυτοῦ λαλεῖν, δῆλόν ἐστιν ὅτι οὐκ ἔχει Πνεῦμα ἅγιον. Τὸ Πνεῦμα τὸ ἅγιον ἀφ' ἑαυτοῦ οὐ λαλήσει, ἀλλ' ὅσα ἀκούσει, ἀναγγελεῖ ὑμῖν· ἀντὶ τοῦ, ἃ ἐλάλησα, ταῦτα βεβαιώσει.—Homil. de Spiritu Sancto. §§ 9, 10: inter CHRYSOSTOMI Op. ed. Bened. Paris. Tom. III. pp. 807, 808.]

the persons, and by scornful disdaining of other to procure yourself authority. What your opinion is of him, your writing declareth; but they which have been of longer and better acquaintance with him than you are, do right well know, and in his behalf do protest, that twenty years since he was able fully to have answered stronger arguments for these matters than any that you have brought at this time. But whatsoever he is to you, God be praised in him, he so liveth as the most malicious of your part cannot justly blame him; and his learning is such, as, when the matter shall be tried, I doubt not but it will fall out, that he with his forty years' age, and such other, whom in like manner you disdain, shall shew more true divinity than a many of your hoar heads and great reading clerks, as you think; whose authority and name alone ye judge sufficient to bear down whatsoever shall be brought against them.

Toward the end, you shew your opinion of real presence of Christ's body in the sacrament, and in that part blame us, as though we had more acquainted ourselves with Ishmael and Hagar (as you say) than with Abraham and Isaac; thereby signifying, that we misdoubted the Almighty power of God in bringing that to pass, which he promiseth or speaketh in the institution of his sacraments. But I must needs judge this to be in you, either ignorant blindness, or hateful malice: blindness, if you do not understand and see, that in this

CAP. XIII.
Of real presence.

controversy we stay not upon God's omnipotency; malice, if you know it and upbraid us with the contrary. We grant as freely as you[1], with Abraham and Isaac, "That God is able to perform whatsoever he doth promise." We grant as freely as you, with the angel, "That no word is impossible to God." We grant as freely as you, with David, "That God hath done whatsoever his will was to do." We grant with the holy Fathers, that a great and marvellous mutation and change is made in the sacrament by the power of God's word[2]. We detest, even as much as you, all such as see no more but common bread or a bare sign in this holy Supper; neither can we think well of you, when you do so falsely charge us with that assertion. But how can you shew, that it was God's holy will to have so many miracles wrought, as you without necessity do make in this sacrament? Yea, and of such sort as be contrary to the manner of all those miracles that the holy Scripture mentioneth to be wrought by his divine

[Rom. iv. 21.]
[Luke i. 37.]
[Ps. cxv. 3.]

[1 See p. 37, above.]
[2 As for instance, in the following passages:—
Οὐ γὰρ ὡς κοινὸν ἄρτον οὐδὲ κοινὸν πόμα ταῦτα λαμβάνομεν· ἀλλ' ὃν τρόπον διὰ λόγου Θεοῦ σαρκοποιηθεὶς Ἰησοῦς Χριστὸς ὁ σωτὴρ ἡμῶν καὶ σάρκα καὶ αἷμα ὑπὲρ σωτηρίας ἡμῶν ἔσχεν, οὕτως καὶ τὴν δι' εὐχῆς λόγου τοῦ παρ' αὐτοῦ εὐχαριστηθεῖσαν τροφὴν, ἐξ ἧς αἷμα καὶ σάρκες κατὰ μεταβολὴν τρέφονται ἡμῶν, ἐκείνου τοῦ σαρκοποιηθέντος Ἰησοῦ καὶ σάρκα καὶ αἷμα ἐδιδάχθημεν εἶναι.—JUST. MART. Apolog. 1. §. 66. Op. ed. Otto, Jen. 1847. Tom. I. p. 156.
Προσλαμβανόμενα τὸν λόγον τοῦ Θεοῦ εὐχαριστία γίνεται, ὅπερ ἐστὶ σῶμα καὶ αἷμα τοῦ Χριστοῦ.—IREN. Adv. hæres. Lib. v. c. 2. Ed. Grabe. Oxon. 1702. p. 400.]

power. Moses turned his rod into a serpent; but all that were present saw that it was a serpent. He made water miraculously to come out of the rock; but all the children of Israel saw and tasted of the water. Christ turned water into wine; but all the company drank and felt it to be wine. The same is to be said of all the residue of marvellous works. And when God's power had miraculously turned these things, that into the which they were turned, reserved and kept that nature that was agreeable to such a thing. The serpent had the very nature of a serpent; the water was of such nature as it behoved water to be; the wine lost not the right nature of wine. Otherwise it may seem rather a juggling than miraculous working. You never read in all the course of the Scripture, that God's power turned the substance of anything, and left the qualities of the other thing that it was before; saving only in this case that you imagine it. God is able to turn darkness into light, and light into darkness; but it were madness to require at God's almighty power to make light, and not to have a shining; that is, to make light to be light and not to be light all at once; or to make light and darkness all one. This were nothing but to pervert the order of God's wisdom. Do you not this in the sacrament, when you appoint the body of Christ to be without quantity, proportion and figure, or to be in a thousand places at once, which is proper only to his divinity? Is not this to take away the nature of a body from his body, and in deed to affirm it to be no body? And yet we say not, but that God is able to work that also, if it be his pleasure. But we say, it was not God's will and pleasure in ordaining the sacrament to have it so. For neither is there any necessity that should constrain him to it, nor doth his Word teach us, that ever he did the like. Oh, ye will say, we must believe Christ's words, "This is my body," which be of as great power now, as they were in the parlour at Jerusalem, to make the very body of Christ really and carnally present; and so the catholic Church (say you) doth teach us. Wherefore upon this verity once settled, divers other things must of necessity follow by drift of reason, although they be not expressly mentioned in Scripture; as the adoration of the sacrament, the turning of the substance of bread and wine, the being of Christ's body in many places at once, &c. Indeed, sir, such is the vanity of man's reason in God's holy mysteries. For when it is once departed from the true sense of God's Word, it draweth in, as it were by links, a number of other absurdities; none of which can have any proof in Scripture, seeing the first root of them came not out of the true sense of Scripture. Even so, when you had devised and given to Christ's words another sense, than the meaning of them doth import, no marvel, if the same reason do lead you to a multitude of other doctrines, not only beside the Word of God, but expressly against it.

Whether that interpretation, that you

make upon these words, do more agree with the Scripture and ground of our faith, than that which we teach, any indifferent man, that is not contentiously bent to the one part or to the other, may easily discern. Your sense is,—when Christ saith, "This is my body," that the natural substance of the bread, which Christ took, was turned into the natural substance of the very body that Christ died in; notwithstanding that the colour, taste, form, and power to nourish, that were before in the substance of bread, doth still remain: and yet under those qualities and accidences of bread is really contained the natural body of Christ, having neither bigness, nor any proportion or sensible quality rightly appertaining to such a body. To express this your meaning, you use to say, that the bread is transubstantiate into the body of Christ. In what tongue or language was it ever seen, in what author was it ever read, that *sum, es, fui,* the verb substantive, might be interpreted by *transubstantiare?* Or if the propriety of the word will not in anywise admit that sense, what one sentence or clause have you in all the course of the bible, that under the like words can receive the like interpretation? Or what proofs can you bring by conference of other places of the Scripture, that these words in this place ought of necessity in this manner to be interpreted? If neither the propriety of the tongue can bear the sense, nor you can bring any examples or proofs out of the word of God, whereupon men in so weighty a matter may stay their consciences, is it not extreme cruelty in you, under pain of damnation to compel them to believe it?

Here you will burden us with the authority of the holy catholic Church, which, as you say, hath alway received and allowed that interpretation. Unto this I answer, that the catholic Church of Christ never generally received the meaning of any sentence, but that they gathered the same, either by examples of the like, or else by grounded reasons, taken out of the Scripture, declared [? declaring] that of necessity it must be so understood. This rule was appointed to the Church by Christ and his apostles; who in their doubts willed men *Scrutari Scripturas*, to search the Scriptures. Therefore when the Church decreed against the Arians and other heretics, that in this sentence, *In principio erat Verbum*, the Word was in the beginning, that *Verbum* was to be taken for the person of the Son of God; or when they decreed, that the Son was *ejusdem substantiæ cum Patre*, of the same substance with the Father; they stayed not only upon their own consent and authority, but brought a great number of proofs out of the Scripture, that it must of necessity be so taken; as it appeareth in Cyril, and other of the holy Fathers. Now then if this that you defend, be the judgment of the catholic Church, it hath undoubtedly good proof in the Scripture; or if you can bring for it no such testimony out of the Word of God, it is evident, that you do wrongfully father this

[John v. 39.]

interpretation upon the holy catholic Church, and under the covert of that name you do promote and set forth your own error. And this much for your opinion.

On the other part, when we interpret Christ's words, we say it is a figurative speech, and such as the Holy Ghost often useth in the institution of sacraments and ceremonies, or in the describing of other mysteries. The figure is named Metonymia; when the name of the thing is given unto the sign. When these words therefore be laid unto us, "This is my body," we say it is most true. But mystically, sacramentally, figuratively, not really and according to the natural substance. For this interpretation we have a number of examples out of the canonical Scriptures. God, speaking of circumcision, saith: "This is my covenant." And yet was circumcision not the covenant indeed, but the sign and testimony, whereby they were assured to be the people of God and partakers of his promises. The Paschal Lamb is called the "Passover;" and yet was it but a testimony and remembrance of the great benefit of God, in passing his plague from them. "This is the victory," saith St Paul, "that overcometh the world, even your faith." And yet is not our faith the victory itself, but the instrument or means whereby the victory is gotten. In like manner divers other places; as, "I am a vine:" "God is a consuming fire:" "The seven kine be seven years:" and that St Paul hath to the Corinthians,—*Petra erat Christus*, "the rock was Christ." And

[Gen. xvii. 10, 13.]

[Exod. xii. 11.]

[1 John v. 4.]

[John xv. 5.]
[Heb. xii. 29.]
[Gen. xli. 26, 27.]

[1 Cor. x. 4.]

yet was not the rock Christ himself really; unless ye will take it, as he there doth in deed, for the spiritual rock. For that spiritual rock was Christ himself, verily and indeed, not only in a mystery or signification. So in the Lord's supper, if you take bread for spiritual bread, as Christ doth in the sixth of John, I will say with you, that it is really and essentially the very true body of Christ itself, and not only mystically. If we had not these many examples with a great number more in the holy Scripture to justify our manner of interpretation, yet the very words which the Spirit of God by singular providence hath used in the evangelist and St Paul, doth manifestly lead us unto this sense, rather than to that you have devised. For in the second part of the sacrament, where Matthew and Mark say, "This is my blood of the new Testament," that Luke and Paul utter in this manner, "This is the new Testament in my blood:" which cannot be otherwise understood, but that this sacrament is a testimony or pledge of his last will and gift of our salvation, confirmed by his most precious blood. Wherefore if you say never so oftentimes with Matthew and Mark,— "This is my body,—This is my blood;" we will repeat as often with Luke and Paul, who were led with the same Spirit,—"This is the new Testament in my body and blood."

This interpretation and meaning of Christ's words, which we gather by conference with other places of holy Scripture,

[Matt. xxvi. 28; Mark xiv. 24.]
[Luke xxii. 20; 1 Cor. xi. 25.]

is confirmed also by the consent of the ancient Fathers in many places: whose testimonies I will recite more copiously; partly, because you seem to signify that they altogether make for you in this matter; partly, that all men may see, how unjustly your sort do term us *figuratores*, because we interpret that sentence by a figure, whereas it is not our device, but the exposition of all the ancient Fathers of the primitive Church. First I will begin with Augustine, *Contra Adimantum*, cap. 12. There it appeareth, that *Adimantus* used Moses's words, *Sanguis est anima*, to make this fond argument:— " Blood is the soul," saith Moses; but "flesh and blood (saith Paul) shall not possess the kingdom of God." Therefore the soul shall not possess the kingdom of God. Augustine's answer to that argument is, that this sentence, *Sanguis est anima*, must be understood figuratively, and not literally, as he in that argument took it. To prove that, he useth these words of Christ, *Hoc est corpus meum;* saying in this wise,—*Possum interpretari illud præceptum in signo positum esse. Non enim dubitavit Dominus dicere, hoc est corpus meum, cum daret signum corporis sui,* " I may (saith Augustine) interpret that precept to consist in a sign or figure. For the Lord doubted not to say, This is my body, when he gave the sign of his body[1]." As if he had said,—in a far greater matter than this, that is, in instituting the sacrament of his death and our

[1 AUGUST. Contr. Adimant. cap. 12. § 3. Op. ed. Bened. Paris. Tom. VIII. col. 124.]

redemption, the Lord doubted not to use a figure, and to say, This is my body, when he gave the sign of his body; therefore this sentence, "Blood is the soul," may sooner be interpreted figuratively. So that the meaning of it is, that blood is the sign of the soul or life, and not the very soul indeed. The same Augustine in his exposition upon the third psalm;—*Judam (inquit) adhibuit ad convivium, in quo corporis et sanguinis sui figuram discipulis suis commendavit.* "He admitted Judas to that feast, wherein he commended to his disciples the figure of his body and blood[1]." The same exposition Tertullian maketh most evidently, in his fourth book against Marcion. *Panem (inquit) acceptum et distributum discipulis corpus suum illum fecit, Hoc est corpus meum dicendo; hoc est, figura corporis mei.* "Christ (saith Tertullian) made that bread, that he took in his hands, and gave to his disciples, his body; saying, This is my body; that is to say, the sign of my body[2]." What can be plainer than this exposition of this ancient father, if men did not study rather to maintain parts, than to confirm truth. His purpose was there to prove against Marcion, that Christ had a true body

[1 Eum [i.e. Judam]...adhibuit ad convivium, in quo corporis et sanguinis sui figuram discipulis commendavit et tradidit.—AUGUST. Enarr. in Psalm. Ps. iii. § 1. Op. ed. cit. Tom. VIII. col. 7.]

[2 Acceptum panem et distributum discipulis corpus suum illum fecit, Hoc est corpus meum dicendo; id est, figura corporis mei. Figura autem non fuisset, nisi veritatis esset corpus.—TERTULL. Adv. Marcion. Lib. IV. c. 40. Op. ed. cit. Vol. I. p. 303.]

indeed, because in the sacrament he ordained the sign or figure of his body; and therefore afterward he addeth,—*Figura autem non esset, nisi veritatis esset corpus.* "That should not be a figure of his body, unless he had a very true body indeed." Augustine again, in 23 Epistle to *Bonifacius: Si (inquit) sacramenta similitudinem quandam earum rerum, quarum sunt sacramenta, non haberent, omnino sacramenta non essent. Ex hac autem similitudine plerumque rerum ipsarum nomina sortiuntur. Sicut ergo secundum quendam modum sacramentum corporis Christi corpus Christi est, et sacramentum sanguinis Christi sanguis Christi est, ita sacramentum fidei fides est.* And a little after,—*Sicut de ipso Baptismo Apostolus, Consepulti (inquit) sumus Christo per baptismum in mortem. Non ait, sepulturam significamus; sed prorsus (inquit) consepulti sumus. Sacramentum ergo tantæ rei, non nisi ejusdem rei vocabulo nuncupavit.* "If sacraments had not a certain similitude of those things, whereof they be sacraments, they should not be sacraments at all. And for this similitude or likeness they commonly have the names of the things themselves. Therefore as the sacrament of Christ's body after a certain fashion is Christ's body; and the sacrament of his blood is his blood; so the sacrament of faith is faith," &c. "As the apostle speaketh of Baptism: 'We be buried,' saith he, 'in death to Christ by baptism.' He saith not, 'we signify burial,' but plainly, 'we be buried.' Therefore he doth nothing else but term the sacrament of so great a thing, by the name of the thing itself[1]." St Augustine's meaning is, to declare to Bonifacius, that Baptism might be called by the name of faith, and that therefore the infant baptized might be truly affirmed to believe, or to have faith, because it had baptism the sacrament of faith. This he proveth by comparison with the sacrament of Christ's body and blood; which, for a similitude or likeness, he saith is called the body and blood of Christ, and that after a certain fashion; adding, that baptism in like manner is faith. And yet no man will be so unwise to say, that baptism is faith in deed really. Wherefore the like is to be judged of the sacrament of the Lord's body, whereby St Augustine proveth it. This also is diligently to be noted, that Augustine saith, all sacraments generally be uttered by name of the things themselves, because of a certain similitude or likeness; and therefore Paul saith not, we signify our burial, but we be buried; calling the sacrament by the name of the thing, as Augustine saith. Again, in *Libro sententiarum Prosperi*,—as it is recited in the decrees, *De consecratione, distinc.* 2. cap. *Hoc est*,—the same Father hath these words:—*Cœlestis panis, qui est caro Christi, suo modo nominatur corpus Christi, cum revera sit sacramentum corporis Christi. Vocaturque ipsa immolatio carnis, quæ sacerdotis manibus fit, Christi passio, mors,*

[1] AUGUST. Ep. 98. § 9. in ed. Bened. Paris. Tom. II. col. 267, 268. The differences of reading are too trivial to need notice.]

crucifixio, non rei veritate sed significante mysterio. "The heavenly bread, which is the flesh of Christ, after a fashion is named the body of Christ: whereas in deed it is but the sacrament of his body. And the offering of the flesh, which is done with the priest's hands, is called the passion, the death, the crucifying of Christ, not in verity of the thing, but in a signifying mystery[2]." The Gloss, in expounding these words of Augustine, saith this. *Cœleste sacramentum, quod vere repræsentat Christi carnem, dicitur corpus Christi, sed improprie; unde dicitur, suo modo, et non rei veritate, sed significante mysterio. Ut sit sensus: vocatur corpus Christi, id est, significat.* "It is called the body of Christ, (saith he,) that is to say, it signifieth the body of Christ[3]."

To this I will add Chrysostom, *Operis imperfecti Homil.* 11. *Si, inquit, vasa sanctificata transferre ad privatos usus peccatum est, in quibus non est verum corpus Christi, sed mysterium corporis Christi continetur, quanto magis vasa corporis nostri, &c.* " If

[2 Sicut ergo cœlestis panis, qui vere Christi caro est, suo modo vocatur corpus Christi, cum revera sit sacramentum corporis Christi, illius videlicet, quod visibile, palpabile, mortale, in cruce est suspensum, vocaturque ipsa immolatio carnis, quæ sacerdotis manibus fit, Christi passio, mors, crucifixio, non rei veritate, sed significante mysterio; sic sacramentum fidei, quod baptismus intelligitur, fides est.—AUGUST. in Libro Sentent. Prosperi, cit. in Gratian. Decret. P. III. De Consecr. dist. 2. c. 48. Corp. Jur. Canon. ed. cit. Vol. I. col. 1180.]

[3 Decret. Gratiani cum Glossis. Paris. 1583. fol. col. 2388, or, Taurini, 1620. fol. col. 1937; both which editions however read—sed non rei veritate, sed significati mysterio.]

(saith he) it be sin to transfer holy vessels unto private uses, in which is not the true body of Christ, but the mystery of his body is contained, how much less should we &c.[1]" What can more plainly declare the figurative sense of those words of Christ, *hoc est corpus meum*, than that Chrysostom saith, "in which vessels is not the very body, but the mystery of it." For if those words were literally to be understanded, (as you say,) then should the holy vessels that contain the sacraments, have in them, not only the mystery of Christ's body and blood, but his very body really in deed; which Chrysostom denieth. In the 83 *Homil. upon Matthew* the same doctor saith, *Si mortuus Jesus non est, cujus symbolum aut signum hoc sacrificium est?* "If Christ be not dead, of whom is this sacrifice a figure and sign[2]?" And upon the twenty-second Psalm:—*Ut quotidie in similitudinem corporis et sanguinis Christi, panem et vinum secundum ordinem Melchisedech nobis ostenderet in sacramento.* "That he might daily shew us in the sacrament bread and wine according to the order of Melchisedech, as the similitude of his body and blood[3]." As before he

[1] Opus imperf. in Matth. hom. XI. Op. ed. Bened. Paris. Tom. VI. App. p. 63. The authorship of the work is doubtful.]
[2] Εἰ γὰρ μὴ ἀπέθανεν ὁ Ἰησοῦς, τίνος σύμβολα τὰ τελούμενα;—CHRYSOST. In Matth. Hom. 82. (al. 83.) § 1. Op. ed. cit. Tom. VII. p. 783.]
[3] Nam vide quid dicit sapientia: sapientia ædificavit sibi domum, supposuit columnas septem, paravit mensam suam, misit servos suos convocans omnes, et dicens: Venite et edite de panibus meis, et bibite vinum quod miscui vobis. Et quia istam mensam

used *symbolum, signum, mysterium*, so he hath here *similitudinem*. Likewise *Dionysius De Ecclesiastica Hierarchia*, cap. 3. *Per venerabilia signa Christus signatur et sumitur*. "By those reverent signs Christ is signified and received[4]." Ambrose also, *De hiis qui initiantur mysteriis*, cap. 9. *Ipse clamat Dominus Jesus, Hoc est corpus meum. Ante benedictionem verborum cœlestium alia species nominatur. Post consecrationem corpus Christi significatur.* "Our Lord Jesus crieth, This is my body. Before the blessing of the heavenly words, one kind is named. After consecration Christ's body is signified[5]." In the fourth book also, *De Sacramentis*, cap. 8, the same Ambrose saith:—*Fac nobis hanc oblationem ascriptam, rationabilem, acceptabilem, quod est figura corporis et sanguinis Domini nostri Jesu Christi.* "Make to us this offering allowable, reasonable, acceptable, which is the figure of the body and blood of our Lord Jesus Christ[6]." Here he acknowledgeth the sa-

præparavit servis et ancillis in conspectu eorum, ut quotidie in similitudinem corporis et sanguinis Christi, panem et vinum secundum ordinem Melchisedech nobis ostenderet in sacramento, ideo dicit: Parasti in conspectu meo mensam, &c.—CHRYSOST. Homil. in Ps xxii et cxvi. Op. ed. Paris. 1588. Tom. I. col. 703. This Homily is not extant in Greek, and is not inserted in the editions of Chrysostom's Works by Savile, Fronto Ducæus, or the Benedictines.]

[4 'Επιτεθέντων τῷ θείῳ θυσιαστηρίῳ τῶν σεβασμίων συμβόλων, δι' ὧν ὁ Χριστὸς σημαίνεται καὶ μετέχεται.—DIONYS. AREOP. De eccles. hierarch. c. 3. § 9. Op. ed. Antw. 1634. Vol. I. p. 295.]

[5 AMBROS. De mysteriis, c. 9. Op. ed. Bened. Paris. Tom. II. col. 339. Quoted in Gratian. Decret. P. 3. De consecr. dist. 2. c. 40.]

[6 De sacram. Lib. IV. cap. 5. Op. ed. ead. Tom.

crament to be a figure. In the sixth book, *De Sacramentis*, cap. 1, he hath these words also:—*Ideo in similitudinem quidem accipis sacramentum, sed veræ naturæ gratiam virtutemque assequeris.* "Therefore thou receivest the sacrament as a similitude, but thou attainest the grace and virtue of the true nature in deed[1]." This sentence of Ambrose containeth our whole doctrine of the sacrament of Christ's body and blood: which is, that it is a figure or sign of his body; and yet not a bare or naked figure, but such a one as thereby we attain in deed the full grace and benefit of his body, that suffered for us and was crucified upon the cross, and have our souls fed and nourished with the same to everlasting life.

Origen upon Matthew saith:—*Panis sanctificatus juxta id, quod habet materiale, in ventrem abit, et in secessum ejicitur, &c.* "The sanctified bread," saith he, "according to that it hath material, passeth into the belly, and is avoided out of the body. But according to the prayer that cometh to it, it is profitable; making that the mind understandeth, and hath regard to that is profitable. Neither is it the matter of the bread, but the word spoken over it, that profiteth him which receiveth it not un-

II. col. 371; where however the word *ratam* is added after *ascriptam*. Quoted in Gratian. Decret. P. 3. De Consecr. dist. 2. c. 55; where the reading is the same as above.]

[1 De Sacram. Lib. VI. c. 1. Op. ed. ead. Tom. II. col. 380; where however for *veræ* and *assequeris* we read *vere* and *consequeris*. Quoted in Gratian. Decret. ib. c. 43. where (ed. cit.) we have *similitudine* and *consequeris*.]

worthily. And thus much have I spoken of the typical and figurative body. Much also may be said of the lively Word itself, which was made flesh and very meat in deed; which meat he that eateth shall surely live for ever: which no ill man can eat, &c.[2]" Here note you, first, that Origen saith, that the matter of the consecrated bread of the sacrament passeth into the belly and is avoided out, expressly against your interpretation of Christ's words, whereby ye say the bread is transubstantiate, and no matter of it left but only accidences. Secondly, that he calleth the sacrament, *Typicum et symbolicum corpus*, "the typical and figurative body." Thirdly, that he affirmeth constantly, that no ill man can eat the very flesh of the second person in Trinity. And yet that is one of the necessary labels that your sort doth teach to depend upon your wrongful interpretation of Christ's words. Wherefore Origen with this one sentence

[2 Εἰ δὲ πᾶν τὸ εἰσπορευόμενον εἰς τὸ στόμα, εἰς κοιλίαν χωρεῖ, καὶ εἰς ἀφεδρῶνα ἐκβάλλεται, καὶ τὸ ἁγιαζόμενον βρῶμα διὰ λόγου Θεοῦ καὶ ἐντεύξεως, κατ' αὐτὸ μὲν τὸ ὑλικὸν, εἰς τὴν κοιλίαν χωρεῖ, καὶ εἰς ἀφεδρῶνα ἐκβάλλεται· κατὰ δὲ τὴν ἐπιγενομένην αὐτῷ εὐχὴν, κατὰ τὴν ἀναλογίαν τῆς πίστεως, ὠφέλιμον γίνεται, καὶ τῆς τοῦ νοῦ αἴτιον διαβλέψεως, ὁρῶντος ἐπὶ τὸ ὠφελοῦν· καὶ οὐχ ἡ ὕλη τοῦ ἄρτου, ἀλλ' ὁ ἐπ' αὐτῷ εἰρημένος λόγος ἐστὶν ὁ ὠφελῶν τὸν μὴ ἀναξίως τοῦ Κυρίου ἐσθίοντα αὐτόν. Καὶ ταῦτα μὲν περὶ τοῦ τυπικοῦ καὶ συμβολικοῦ σώματος. Πολλὰ δ' ἂν καὶ περὶ αὐτοῦ λέγοιτο τοῦ Λόγου, ὃς γέγονε σὰρξ, καὶ ἀληθινὴ βρῶσις, ἥν τινα ὁ φαγὼν πάντως ζήσεται εἰς τὸν αἰῶνα, οὐδενὸς δυναμένου φαύλου ἐσθίειν αὐτήν.—ORIG. Comment. in Matth. Tom. XI. § 14. Op. ed. Delarue, Paris. 1740. Tom. III. pp. 499, 500.]

teareth off divers of your counterfeited labels, that you stitch to Christ's testaments by drift of reason, without the warrant of his holy word. Moreover, Augustine, *De Doctrina Christ.* Lib. III. cap. 9, after he hath declared, that in the New Testament God hath left unto his people but few sacraments and ceremonies, and the same to be understanded not carnally and servilely according to the letter; and there for example hath mentioned baptism and the celebration of the Lord's body and blood; in the end he addeth these words: "In which," saith he, "as, to follow the letter, and to take the signs for those things that are signified by them, is a point of servile infirmity; so, to interpret the signs evil, is the point of wandering error[1]." As he counteth it a fond and wicked error, not to interpret the signs well and according to God's word, so by a straight literal sense to take the signs for the things signified, he esteemeth a servile infirmity. What can be more plainly spoken against that interpretation that you make upon these words of Christ; whereby you do bind us to a servile and literal sense of this word, "Is," and in such sort take the signs of this sacrament for the things signified, as you affirm bread and wine (which St Augustine and the other doctors call the external signs,) clean to be turned into the body and blood of Christ? The same Augustine

[1 Ut autem literam sequi, et signa pro rebus quæ iis significantur accipere, servilis infirmitatis est; ita inutiliter signa interpretari, male vagantis erroris est.—AUGUST. De Doctr. Christian. Lib. III. c. 9. Op. ed. Bened. Paris. Tom. III. P. 1. col. 49.]

Contra Adimantum Manich.:—" The Lord saith, 'This is my body,' when he gave the sign of his body[2]." Also upon the xcviii. Psalm he speaketh in this manner :—" Ye shall not eat that body that you see, nor ye shall not drink that blood that they shall shed. It is a mystery, that I tell you; which shall relieve you, if you understand it spiritually[3]."

Will you not yet understand, from whence our men received this interpretation? Will you not yet perceive, that we sucked not it out of our own fingers, but were led unto it by the testimonies of holy Scriptures and teaching of these ancient Fathers? Will you not cease unjustly to burden us, that we cavil and dally upon tittles and syllables; whereas yourself in this sentence would drive us to such an understanding of this one syllable, "Is," as the like is not in the whole Bible?

But ye will allege for yourself, as you signify in your writing, that Ambrose, Cyprian, Chrysostom, and other ancient Fathers have in this case used the terms of transmutation, alteration, conversion, transelementation, &c.: whereby they have plainly declared their meaning to be as yours is; and that

[2 See note, p. 201. above.]
[3 Ille [i. e. Jesus] autem instruxit eos, et ait illis, Spiritus est qui vivificat, caro autem nihil prodest: verba quæ locutus sum vobis, spiritus est et vita. Spiritaliter intelligite quod locutus sum: non hoc corpus quod videtis, manducaturi estis; et bibituri illum sanguinem, quem fusuri sunt qui me crucifigent. Sacramentum aliquod vobis commendavi: spiritaliter intellectum vivificabit vos.—AUGUST. Enarr. in Psal. xcviii. § 9. Op. ed. ead. Tom. IV. col. 1066.]

no bread there remaineth, but only the substance of Christ's body. True it is indeed, that those holy Fathers used such words, not for that they were of your opinion, but only to the end they might more reverently, as meet was, and more lively express the dignity and effect of that heavenly mystery; wherein Jesus Christ, by his infallible promise, unfeignedly giveth to the faith of his people the very fruition of his body and blood, with the whole benefit of his precious death and passion, and by the working of the Holy Ghost marvellously joineth us in one body together with him. Is not this, think you, a marvellous change, and to man's estimation a miraculous work; when, by the power of the Holy Ghost and word of God, of common bread and wine, such as we daily feed our bodies with, is made the dreadful and reverend sacraments and mysteries of Jesus Christ; whereby (as I said) he doth, not by a bare sign only, but verily and indeed endow his faithful people, and make them partakers of his body and blood? Yea, and that in such sort, that even as truly as the bread doth nourish our body, and even as truly as the wine doth comfort our spirits, so truly and unfeignedly doth the heavenly food of his body and blood, torn and shed for us, by faith, in time of that holy supper, nourish, strengthen, and comfort our soul; and, by the wonderful working of his Spirit, make our bodies also apt to resurrection. Truly when I earnestly consider the effect of this sacrament, as it must needs be by the truth of Christ's promises, I confess I am not able with words to utter so much as in my mind I do conceive, and together withal eschew the absurdity of your real presence and transubstantiation. Wherefore I marvel not, if those holy Fathers, fearing no such inconveniences, but looking rather pithily to express the thing, did use those earnest words and manners of speaking; and yet meant not as you now of their words do gather. Although no similitude can sufficiently declare the thing, I will, for the simpler sort, so much as I can, endeavour by a comparison to set forth that I do conceive. If a temporal prince, for certain causes moving him, would give you a thousand pound land by the year, and for that purpose had caused the writings to be made; the same writing, until it be confirmed by the prince, is nothing but common parchment and ink framed into letters by some inferior man's hand, neither doth it bring any effect; but when the prince hath once added to his seal, and confirmed the grant, it is no more called parchment, or common writing, but the king's letters-patents; and now hath that reverence, that all to whom they be shewed, do vail their bonnets, as bringing with it some part of the prince's majesty. Such a change is now made in those trifling things, that before no man esteemed. You also, to whom this land should be given, would not think this writing common parchment blotted with ink, but the perfect deed of your prince, whereby you were assuredly possessed of the foresaid lands. Moreover, when the prince, at the delivery of the same, should say, Sir, here is a thousand pound land that I give freely to you and to your heirs, I think you would not be so fond to think, either that the prince doth mock you, because you see not the lands presently, or else to conceive with yourself, that you have the lands really inclosed within the compass of your writing. For the king's authority in the writing giveth you as full possession of the lands as though you held them, if it were possible, in your hand. And you in this case might justly say to your friend, shewing your letters-patents, Lo, here is a thousand pound land that my prince hath given me. If then there be so great a change made in framing the covenant and deed of an earthly prince; if his seal do bring such force and effect to his gift and letters-patents; how much more marvellous change, alteration, or transmutation, must we think it to be, when the base creatures of bread and wine be consecrated into the sacrament of the everlasting covenant and testament of Jesus Christ; wherein he giveth us, not earthly vanities, but the precious food of his body and blood, remission of sins, and the heritage of his heavenly kingdom! how much more of effect must this sacrament be, that is sealed with the promise and words of our Saviour Christ, who is truth itself, and cannot deceive any that trusteth in him! Wherefore, to express this change of the external elements into so heavenly mysteries; to shew the effect of this sacrament; to withdraw the ignorant minds of the people from the profane cogitation of a bare sign in this matter, the ancient Fathers had good cause to use such words. And yet therein do they nothing at all defend your miraculous works, that you devise to be made in the Lord's supper.

As for the similitude wherewith you would declare the necessity of your labels, depending upon the first founded absurdity, it is both of as small force as other that you before used, and you handle it with more sluttish eloquence than is meet for such a matter as this is. For the drawing of the capons, the scumming of the pot, the stinking water, the hewing of wood, the putting on the broach with guts, garbage and all, &c., be phrases and terms more meet for the kitchen than for the divinity-school; and such as yourself, I think, would not have used, if your mocking spirit had not so ravished you, as you wist not what you did. If we had resembled your labels, which you cut out by drift of reason, unto so base matters, you would have said, that we had railed, and done otherwise than it became us. But since yourself doth so take them, we must think, that God oftentimes moveth his adversaries to utter truth against themselves. But if the same master, that you imagine to command his servant to make ready that he may dine, did mean only that he should set upon the table such cold meat as was in the house, because he saw no cause or necessity of greater provision, and the servant, upon his own foolish head, would mistake his master's commandment, and conceiving that he would have great strangers, did kill his capons, chickens, and other provision about his house, and busied himself, with more labour than thank, to make them ready; do you not think, I pray you, that he might justly be counted an unprofitable servant and worthy by correction to be taught more wit, for that he putteth his master to greater charges, and himself to more pains, than the matter required, if he had rightly understanded his master's will and commandment? Even so, sir, those things that you say followeth by force of reason and argument upon the first sentence, do follow indeed only upon that sense that yourself doth imagine, mistaking your master's will and pleasure; and not upon that meaning that Christ himself would have his words to be taken in. For all that he would have done may be sufficiently done without the working of so many miracles, as you in this case would drive his omnipotency unto. Wherefore we are not so much to be blamed for mistrusting the almighty power of God, which we confess to be in all things, that his pleasure is to have it shewn [by], as you are for presuming upon the same to have miracles wrought beside his will and without necessity. For by the means of your manifold miracles, without the express word of God, whereupon men's faith in such matters should be grounded, you make that sacrament a torment to try men's weak and feeble consciences; which Christ ordained to be a comfortable and spiritual feeding, to increase and strengthen the consciences of christian people.

This have I thought good to answer [to] your defence of private mass; and, as a champion not meet to match with any great clerk, yet in such sort as I could, to resist your assault, that you make upon the foresaid protestation, not as good David valiantly assaulted Goliath in defence of his prince and country, but as amorous Paris traiterously shot at Achilles in the behalf of his love Helena. For neither is it Goliath that you fight against in his bravery, as you say, bragging against the people of God, but rather Achilles manfully revenging the incest committed with the spouse of Christ, which with your amorous cups you have allured from him; nor yet do you come stoutly as David did in the name of the living God, before the face of both the armies to hurl your stones, but privily out of a corner shoot your arrows against him, as Paris against Achilles. You were afraid, perhaps, if he had seen you, that, with shame enough, he would have wrung your bow and arrows out of your hand; but truly I think, he would not have so done, but rather, knowing that in this quarrel he could not be wounded, he would have suffered you to shoot your fill, and with his naked hand receiving your blunt arrows, in such sort would have picked them at your face, as for shame either you should have run out of the place, or at the least submitted yourself and yielded to the truth,

that you protest yourself to have forsaken.
Wherefore as you have the fear of God, as
you have care of your soul's health, I most
earnestly exhort you to leave study of contention; and with a single heart diligently
to ponder the reasons on both parts as the
weight of the matter requireth. Consider,
as the holy father Cyprian counselleth[1], of
what authority Christ's institution ought to
be; that we should not be so bold to alter
any part of those weighty and great precepts
that so nighly touch the sacrament of our
salvation. Consider that neither Christ's
ordinance, nor the testimony of St Paul,
maketh any signification of sole receiving,
or ministering under one kind, but all contrarywise. Consider that Justin[2], Dionysius[3], Cyprian[4], the holy council of Nice[5],
with all other the ancient Fathers, testify the
common manner of the primitive Church to
have been in form of a communion and that
in both kinds. Consider that Chrysostom[6]
and other so earnestly call the people being
present unto it, as they affirm them to do
impudently that do refrain. Consider that
the manner of the primitive Church was, as
Dionysius[7] witnesseth, that none did remain
in the church, but those only that would
communicate. Consider that Anacletus[8],

[1 See note p. 162, above.]
[2 See note, p. 81, above.]
[3 See note, p. 83, above.]
[4 See notes, pp. 33, 4, and 75, and 140, above.]
[5 See note, pp. 30, 31, above, and our author's remarks on it, pp. 157, 8.]
[6 See notes, pp. 68 and 107, above.]
[7 See note, p. 83, above.]
[8 See note, p. 128, above.]

Sixtus[9], the canons of the Apostles[10] and Antioch[11] council threatened excommunication and punishment to such as, being present at consecration and reading of the lessons of Scripture, would not receive. Consider, I say, and unfeignedly weigh these things with yourself, and ye cannot choose but see, that the authority of God's word and consent of the primitive Church maketh wholly with us in these matters. And on the contrary part you shall perceive, that you have no colour in the Scripture for private mass; that you are fain to seek defence in the Church's authority beside God's word; that your reasons be grounded on false principles and such as have no proof at all; that your authorities out of the doctors be either abuses of the primi-

[9 This is a misprint, I conceive, for *Calixtus*, to whom our author has referred above, in connexion with Anacletus, on this point; in consequence of the testimony attributed to Calixtus in the early editions of Gratian's Decree, P. 3. De Cons. dist. 2. c. 10. See p. 128, above.]

[10 Πάντας τοὺς εἰσιόντας πιστοὺς, καὶ τῶν γραφῶν ἀκούοντας, μὴ παραμένοντας δὲ τῇ προσευχῇ καὶ τῇ ἁγίᾳ μεταλήψει, ὡς ἀταξίαν ἐμποιοῦντας τῇ ἐκκλησίᾳ, ἀφορίζεσθαι χρή.—APOSTOL. Canon. ix.; Concil. ed. Hardouin. Paris. 1715. Tom. I. col. 12. Quoted in Gratian. Decret. P. 3. De Consecr. dist. 1. c. 62. It is variously numbered in different editions as Can. 7, 9, & 10.]

[11 Πάντας τοὺς εἰσιόντας εἰς τὴν ἐκκλησίαν τοῦ Θεοῦ, καὶ τῶν ἱερῶν γραφῶν ἀκούοντας, μὴ κοινωνοῦντας δὲ εὐχῆς ἅμα τῷ λαῷ, ἢ ἀποστρεφομένους τὴν μετάληψιν τῆς εὐχαριστίας κατά τινα ἀταξίαν· τούτους ἀποβλήτους γίνεσθαι τῆς ἐκκλησίας, ἕως ἂν ἐξομολογησάμενοι καὶ δείξαντες καρποὺς μετανοίας, καὶ παρακαλέσαντες, τυχεῖν δυνηθῶσι συγγνώμης.—CONCIL. ANTIOCH. (a. 341.) Can. 2.; Concil. ed. Hardouin. Tom. I. col. 593, 4.]

tive Church, or such extraordinary cases of necessity, contrary to the common manner, as they cannot be rules to shew either what was then orderly done, or what now ought of right to be done.

Be not these gay reasons, think you, to build men's consciences upon? Private mass is nothing but sole receiving in case of necessity; therefore it is lawful. The priest may celebrate alone in the assembly of the people, because divers in necessity and extremity received alone in their private houses. The priest may receive alone when the people will not, because he is bound to offer, and the people is left free. The priest may do it when he will, because he may do it in necessity when the people will not. The minister may receive alone, for company is but an ornament, and not of the substance of the sacrament. The doctors in divers places name one kind; therefore one kind only was received of the people. How will you be able to prove, that private mass is nothing but sole receiving in necessity? How will you be able to prove, that it is all one thing for the minister in the congregation, and a lay man at home in peril to receive alone? How will you prove, that the priest is bound to the frequenting of the sacrament, and the people left free? How will you prove, that company is but an accident or ornament to the sacrament, or that one kind only was received, because one kind only was named? And yet these arguments must be good, or else those proofs and testimonies that you would have to seem invincible, shall indeed be of no force.

O sir, for the love of God, weigh the matter more indifferently. Do not dissemble that you must needs know. If you will have your doctrine tried by the balance of the Scripture and primitive Church, add more weight to your side of the balance, or else confess that your part is the lighter. Let not the vain sound of the holy Church's name, where the thing is not, lead you to be enemy to that doctrine, which you see to have more force in the Word of God. Remember that the true Church is ruled and guided only by Christ's word and doctrine. "If you abide (saith he) in my word, then be you my true disciples." Christ is the good shepherd, and the Church is the fold of his right sheep. Christ is the wise master, and the Church is the company of his diligent scholars. Christ is the bridegroom and the Church is his dearly beloved spouse. The true Church, therefore, will not go ranging what way she lusteth; she will not learn of her own brain; she will not follow her own phantasy. They be wild goats, they be not tame sheep, that when the shepherd's voice calleth one way, will run headlong another way. They be self-will moichers[1], they be not diligent scholars, that, leaving their master's teaching, will follow their own

[John viii. 31.]

[[1] I give this word as spelt in the original, not being sure what is intended by it. Possibly the phrase intended may be *self-will mouchers*, from the old word *mouch*, signifying *to swallow greedily*.]

interpretations. She is a froward and presumptuous woman, she is not an obedient wife, that will make light of her husband's commandments, and think she may alter them at her pleasure. The true sheep of Christ therefore, the diligent scholars, the obedient spouse, that is, the right and true Church, will hearken only to her good Shepherd's voice, will follow her Master's precepts, will obey her Husband's commandments. How then can you excuse yourself by your holy mother the Church, if you teach otherwise than Christ hath taught, and make such interpretations, of your own head, as have no ground in his holy Word? You do under that name maintain your own error; ye follow not the Church's authority. If you will hearken to Christ's Church, to the apostles' Church, to the old Fathers' Church, neither Christ, nor the Apostles, nor the Fathers teach you any such thing. And so ye seem yourself in a sort to confess, or else ye would never strive so much for unwritten verities, and authority of the Church in doctrines beside God's word. You needed no such helps, if your teaching had just proof in the Scripture and ancient Fathers, as indeed it hath not.

This [Thus] have I framed my answer unto you in such sort, as I trust the indifferent reader may judge, that my mind and purpose is, rather directly and plainly to confute the sum of your untrue doctrine, than, as you do, to seek shifts by cavilling to discredit my adversary. For if I should have scanned every syllable, word, or sentence, that in this writing hath passed you, and endeavoured captiously to have taken advantage at every trifle, (as your sort is wont to deal with us for fault of better matter,) both I should have fallen into that fault that I protest myself to mislike in you, and my answer would have grown to such a length, as it might justly have wearied the reader. I have therefore meddled only with the principal points of this your Apology, which may seem to be of chief force in those matters that you touch: and of purpose have let pass many small trifles, wherein both you might justly have been reproved, and some men, I know, will think meet and worthy to be answered. I will now end, and cease any further to exhort you to a more diligent examining and discussing of the residue of your doctrines; trusting that your own conscience, having now more fear of God than you say you had before, will drive you to the same. Which I pray God may be, if not by this occasion, yet by some other, when his holy will shall be.

FINIS.[1]

[[1] The colophon is,—Imprynted at London in Fleetestreete, by Thomas Powell.]

ERRATUM.

P. 30. *note*, l. 1, 2. For *Dionysius Exiguus* read *Isidorus Mercator*.

INDEX

OF

AUTHORS CITED OR REFERRED TO.

Ambrose. 27. 75, 6. 96. 102. 133. 140. 191. 207-8. 211.
Anacletus. 128. 218.
Apostles, canons of. 219.
Augustine. 7. 91. 93. 94, 5. 101. 120, 1. 146. 148. 184. 186, 7. 188. 201-5. 210, 1.
Basil. 38. 141.
Bede. 121.
Bernard. 184, 5.
Calixtus. 219.
Chrysostom. 13-6. 54. 68. 78. 84. 94. 99-101. 103. 104-7. 129. 142, 3. 187. 191, 2. 205-7. 211. 218.
—— Liturgy of. 97.
Clemens Alexandrinus. 88, 9. 91. 146.
—— Romanus. 151, 2.
Constantine, Donation of. 170, 1.
Cornelius Papa. 159.
Council, of Antioch. 219.
—— Basil. 39.
—— Constance. 38.
—— Eliberis (Elvira). 102.
—— Florence. 39.
—— Gangra. 127.
—— Lateran. 38.
—— Nice. 29. 30, 1. 153. 157. 218.
—— Rome. 39.
—— in Trullo. 159.
—— Valence. 39.
Cyprian. 24. 33, 4. 54. 62. 74, 5. 80. 84. 96. 109, 10. 115. 121.
122. 124. 129. 131, 2. 136. 139. 140. 143. 150. 159. 161, 2. 165, 6. 190. 211. 218.
Cyril (Alex.) 25, 6. 124. 149. 198.
Dionysius Areopagita. 20. 54. 82, 3. 207. 218.
—— Exiguus. 30.
Erasmus. 22. 123.
Eusebius. 28. 92. 153. 156. 159.
Gelasius. 138. 159.
Gratian. 121. 137. 138. 151. 159. 205. 208. 219.
Gregorius Nazianzenus. 141.
Hilary. 141. 183, 4.
Ignatius. 67.
Irenæus. 89. 90. 91, 2. 194.
Isidorus Mercator. 223. (30.)
Isychius. 150.
Jerome. 126. 142. 189. 190.
Jewel, Bishop. 4. 45. 50. 192.
Julius Papa. 137.
Justin Martyr. 54. 81. 90. 125. 129. 146. 156. 194. 218.
Leo Magnus. 70.
Luther. 166.
Melancthon. 166, 7.
Origen. 124. 147. 149. 189. 208, 9.
Sergius Papa. 77.
Socrates. 121. 127.
Sozomen. 121.
Tertullian. 23. 62. 89. 124. 129. 133. 139. 147. 202.
Theodoret. 140.

THE END.

www.ingramcontent.com/pod-product-compliance
Lightning Source LLC
Chambersburg PA
CBHW070311230426
43663CB00011B/2085